sutekina okashi

more treats from Keiko's Kitchen

keiko ishida

mc Marshall Cavendish
Cuisine

Editor: Lydia Leong
Designer: Lorraine Aw
Food stylist: Keiko Ishida
Photographer: Takehisa Ishida

© 2017 Marshall Cavendish International (Asia) Private Limited

Published by Marshall Cavendish Cuisine
An imprint of Marshall Cavendish International

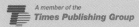
A member of the
Times Publishing Group

Other Marshall Cavendish Offices:
Marshall Cavendish Corporation. 99 White Plains Road, Tarrytown NY 10591-9001,
USA • Marshall Cavendish International (Thailand) Co Ltd. 253 Asoke, 12th Flr,
Sukhumvit 21 Road, Klongtoey Nua, Wattana, Bangkok 10110, Thailand • Marshall
Cavendish (Malaysia) Sdn Bhd, Times Subang, Lot 46, Subang Hi-Tech Industrial Park,
Batu Tiga, 40000 Shah Alam, Selangor Darul Ehsan, Malaysia

Marshall Cavendish is a registered trademark of Times Publishing Limited

National Library Board, Singapore Cataloguing-in-Publication Data

Names: Ishida, Keiko, 1965-
Title: Sutekina okashi : more treats from Keiko's kitchen / Keiko Ishida.
Description: Singapore : Marshall Cavendish Cuisine, [2017]
Identifiers: OCN 987146820 | 978-981-47-7170-2 (paperback)
Subjects: LCSH: Desserts--Japan. | Cooking, Japanese. | LCGFT: Cookbooks.
Classification: DDC 641.860952--dc23

Printed by Markono Print Media Pte Ltd

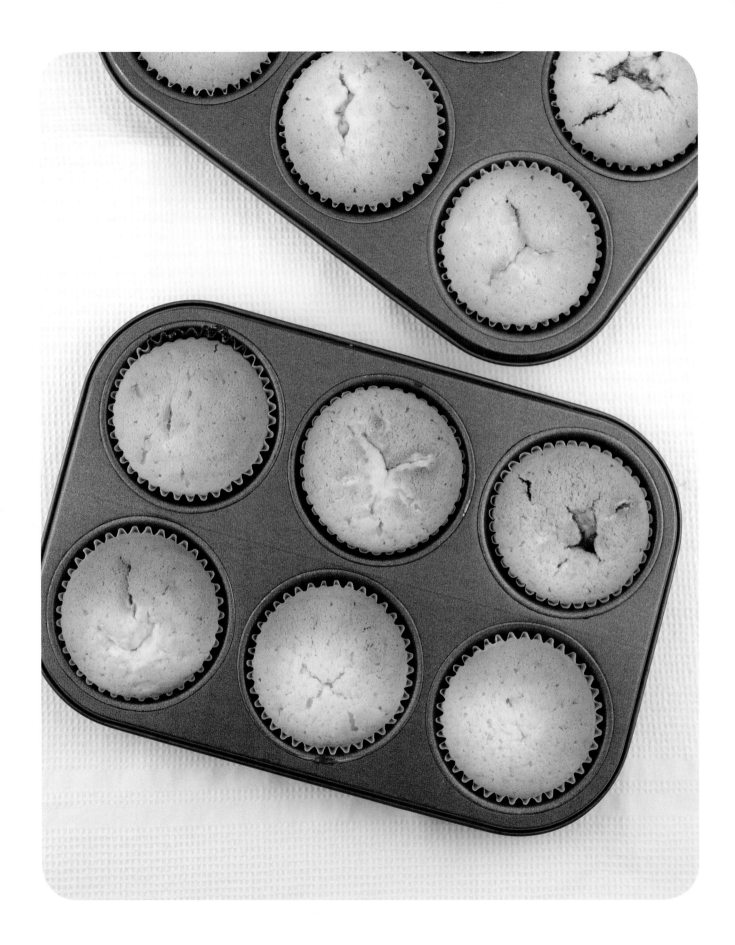

contents

acknowledgements

I would like to thank:

My baking teacher, Ms. Chie Kato. When my first book, *Okashi: Sweet Treats Made with Love*, was published, she was so happy for me. Whenever I was unsure if I should continue as a baking instructor, she always encouraged me saying, "You make such wonderful sweets, you should continue." She has been influential in my baking, and I thank her from the bottom of my heart.

All my students from all over the world. They have been my motivation in my journey as a baking instructor. The students from Shermay's Cooking School (now closed), who gave me the courage to teach in English. Despite my imperfect English, they listened patiently and became a fan of my sweets. In particular, Ms. Clare Wee, Ms. Susan Utama, Ms. Emily Cheng, Ms. Law Siew Khee, Ms. Lin Limei and Mr. Loke Kah Yin, who attended my first class taught in English. This book would not have been possible without them.

Ms. Shermay Lee, owner of Shermay's Cooking School where I conducted baking classes in Singapore. She taught me to face the challenges in my life, and for that, I will always be grateful.

Ms. Mami Gunji, Ms. Chizuko Usui, Ms. Mayumi Yashiro and Ms. Junko Suzuki. Despite their busy schedules, they gave me their precious weekends. They baked with me and shared their ideas. Also, my close friend, Ms. Ayumi Kuwabara, who helped me get groceries on so many occasions. Thank you so much.

Ms. Asuka Yokoyama and Ms. Midori Mills, who helped me with my English and did not give up on me.

Ms. Umika Matsushita, who taught me the link between astrology and herbal therapy. When I first shared with her my idea about making astrological herbal treats, she loved it and wanted to try the recipes, giving me a positive push.

Ms. Lydia Leong, my editor, who trusted me enough to give me this project, with only online communication between us, since I am based in Japan and she in Singapore. Thank you for taking on this adventure to publish my second book.

My parents, for always loving me and supporting me in whatever I do.

My loving husband, Takehisa Ishida. He took on the challenge of taking the photographs for this book and produced many beautiful pictures. He juggled his time between work and this project, and did not take a break for 2 months. We had our ups and downs, but in the end, the experience became a fulfilling and harmonious one. Thank you for your support and for always being there.

Last but not least, I would also like to express my love and gratitude to you for choosing this book. Thank you for finding a place for it in your baking. May you create many happy moments in life through *sutekina okashi* baking!

Much love,

Keiko

introduction

It has been seven years since my first book, *Okashi: Sweet Treats Made with Love*, was published in Singapore in 2009. That was my first attempt to document all the sweets I have been making since childhood. It was unbelievable for me, being born and raised in Japan, to produce a book in English. Shocking as it was, this extraordinary event led me to think it was meant to be. The book continues to be a bestseller and it clinched an award at the Gourmand World Cookbook Awards that year. Now, I'm extremely happy to present to you my second book in English, *Sutekina Okashi: More Treats from Keiko's Kitchen*.

The Japanese word, *sutekina*, means lovely or charming, and *okashi* refers to home-made sweet treats. It is my hope that when you present your loved ones and friends with treats made using recipes from this book, they will exclaim, "Wow! What a lovely treat!" ("*Sutekina okashi!*")

In *Okashi*, I shared basic recipes. In this book, I share recipes that are more exquisite in taste and appearance. It is my hope that you will use your skills honed from making the treats in *Okashi* to create these new treats in *Sutekina Okashi*.

In the first section, New Creations, you will find western-style treats made using popular Japanese ingredients such as green tea, red bean paste and soy bean powder. I hope you will enjoy these flavours as much as I do.

The second section features all-time favourites. Although the treats may seem familiar, I add a Japanese touch to the recipes, including using Japanese techniques for softer textures and using less sugar.

In the third section, I invite you into the world of good luck treats. This is a marriage of herbal therapy and astrology, both of which I have a deep interest in. Just for fun, try them out on yourself, family and friends.

I don't have my own patisserie nor am I a highly skilled chef. And for those of you who are like me, we can in our own way, make simple, tasty treats straight out of the oven, the home-baking way. It's possible with decoration and presentation to make refined treats from simple recipes. And most importantly, these treats can bring happiness to our loved ones and friends.

The scent of baking in the kitchen is like aromatherapy. The smell of lemon, butter and custard when whisking lemon curd is so tempting. These are just simple examples of how wonderful it is to bake.

May this book inspire you to bake and bring tons of joy and happiness to you and those around you.

With love from a small kitchen near the sea,

Keiko

baking basics

THINGS TO DO BEFORE YOU START BAKING

1

Read the recipe and understand it

Read the recipe through and make sure you understand it before you start baking. Take note of the ingredients and equipment you will need, and be aware of the time required for putting the recipe together, so you can plan your time.

2

Prepare the ingredients and equipment needed

Make sure you have all the necessary ingredients and equipment on hand before attempting a recipe. As far as possible, always use the freshest and highest quality of ingredients you can find. Weigh the ingredients in advance. I recommend using a digital scale which enables you to measure out ingredients accurately. Some recipes require advance preparation such as bringing ingredients to the right temperature, greasing and lining cake pans, sifting flour, separating eggs yolks from whites, melting chocolate or butter and toasting nuts, which should be done to make the baking process smoother. Once done, you will find that you are halfway through to completing the recipe!

3

Have a neat, clean work space

To work more efficiently, you need a neat and clean space. If your kitchen is small and tends to become overheated like mine, expand your working area with an extra table in the dining room outside the kitchen.

4

Check and adjust the room temperature, if necessary

Room temperature and level of humidity affects the outcome of your baking. If necessary, turn on your air conditioner to lower the temperature and level of humidity.

5

Preheat the oven and create space in the refrigerator and freezer

Make preheating the oven before you start baking a habit. It is fine to let some cakes and cookies sit while the oven warms up, but it is always best to put them into the oven the moment the batter has been mixed. If a cake needs to be cooled down or chilled, make space in the refrigerator or freezer beforehand.

baking equipment

1 Chiffon cake pan or tube pan

This cake pan is made up of two aluminium pieces—an outer ring and a base piece that forms the bottom and the centre tube. It is not advisable to use a non-stick tube pan when baking chiffon cake.

2 Fluted tart tin with removable base / fluted tartlet tins

In my recipes, I often use tart tins that are either 20 cm or 22 cm in diameter. A tart or pie this size will typically serve 8–10 persons. I also used fluted tartlet tins for making miniature treats. These miniature tins are available in a variety of shapes at kitchenware shops.

3 Aluminium weights

Aluminium weights are reusable and can be easily washed and cleaned after use. When blind- baking tart shells, line the tart tin with aluminium foil or a non-stick baking mat, pressing well into the bottom corners, then add the baking weights. Other types of baking weights include ceramic weights, dried beans or rice.

4 Muffin pan and paper muffin cases / muffin cups

My oven is small, so I use a 6-hole muffin pan instead of a 12-hole pan. That is why my muffin recipes only make 6 muffins, but you can double the recipe to make more. I also use individual muffin cups of the same size for baking muffins. I line the pan or cups with paper cases as this makes it easier to remove the muffins after baking.

5 Pound cake pans

When baking pound cakes, you can use any type of pound cake pans from those made of tin, aluminium or stainless steel. Take note however, that tin pans absorb heat easily and will not be ideal if making chilled desserts such as mousse cakes and cheesecakes.

6

Round cake pans / round cake pan with removable base / cake ring and bottom plate

These are used for baking layered sponge cakes, butter cakes, cheesecakes and more. A cake pan with a base (6a) is useful when baking cakes in a water bath. A cake pan with a removable base (6b) allows the cake to be easily removed from the pan. A cake ring (6c) is used for making mousse cakes and it is always used with a bottom plate. In this book, I used small cake rings when baking galette bretonnes to help the buttery galettes keep their shape while baking.

7

Square cake pans

These are useful for baking layered sponge cakes, butter cakes and brownies. Square cake are easy to slice more evenly. In my recipes, I often use 18-cm, 20-cm and 24-cm square pans.

8

Swiss roll cake pan

A Swiss roll cake pan is a shallow square pan typically made of aluminium or stainless steel. They come in a variety of sizes.

9

Ovenproof dish / ramekins

These are heat-resistant ceramic baking moulds that can be baked in and brought to the table directly without the need to transfer to a serving plate.

10

Fancy moulds

In this book, I used a variety of moulds such as a daisy-shaped silicone mould (10a), Bundt pan (10b), Gugelhupf pan (10c), ring pan (10d), half spherical rectangular pan (10e) and jelly moulds (10f). Fancy moulds produce prettier cakes. When you want to know the volume of the mould, pour water into the mould and weigh the water. This will give you the volume of the mould.

11

Metal cookie cutters (plain and fluted)

I prefer using metal cookie cutters to plastic ones, as I find that metal ones give a cleaner cut which is important for pies and scones, as it makes them rise better. I recommend getting a boxed set that includes cutters in a range of sizes. You can find many fancy cookie cutters in various shapes, such as hearts, stars, animals and flowers. In this book, I used a gingerbread man cookie cutter for cutting ginger cookies.

1

4

3

2

6c

5

6b

6a

Piping tips

12a Round, plain 5-mm and 10-mm tips: These are used for piping batter into small moulds, as well as piping line biscuits and choux pastry.

12b Star and drop flower tips: Star tips can be used for fancy decorations like stars, shell shapes and zig-zag lines. Drop flower tips can be used to pipe pretty flower shapes easily. I used it for piping the raspberry chiffon cake in this book.

12c Petal and leaf decorating tips: These are used for making flower petals. Choose the tips according to the size you want for your flowers.

Piping bags

Piping bags are essential for decorating cakes. They are also useful for piping cake batter into small cake pans and mousse into glasses. Both disposable plastic piping bags and reusable piping bags are available. I like to use 35-cm piping bags.

Flower nail

A flower nail is essential for piping flowers. The key to making perfect butter cream or sugar flowers is to coordinate the turning of the nail with the formation of each petal.

Digital scale

Since precise measurements are very important in baking, I recommend using a digital scale. I prefer using a scale that has a minimum scale unit of less than 1 g and which can weigh up to 3 kg for home baking.

Measuring spoons

To measure small quantities of ingredients precisely, use measuring spoons. It is ideal to have a set made up of $1/4$ tsp, $1/3$ tsp, $1/2$ tsp, 1 tsp, $1/2$ Tbsp and 1 Tbsp sizes. Note that 1 tsp = 5 ml and 1 Tbsp = 15 ml. When measuring dry ingredients such as salt and baking powder, be sure to level them off. When measuring liquids such as vanilla extract and liqueur, pour the liquid until it reaches the edge of the spoon.

Measuring cups

Use clear measuring cups, preferably made of microwave-safe glass, so you can read the measurements at eye level and heat the liquid if necessary. I find it useful to have a 250-ml cup and a 500-ml cup on hand. I also weigh liquids using a digital scale especially when dividing small amounts of mixtures among moulds.

10a

10b

10c

10d

10f

10e

11

7

8

9

17

18 Wire sieve

A wire sieve is necessary for sifting flour. I use one that is 16 cm in diameter. It is also useful for straining liquid mixtures. Small wire sieves can be used to dust icing sugar or cocoa powder on cakes, pastries and other desserts.

19 Mixing bowls

Stainless steel bowls are useful for recipes that require setting a bowl over hot or iced water since they conduct heat well. They are easily washed and kept clean, and are very durable. I recommend keeping two 18-cm bowls, two 23-cm bowls and one 27-cm bowl on hand for baking.

20 Whisks

Choose stainless-steel whisks with fine and solid wires. My preference is for 27-cm and 35-cm long whisks.

21 Electric cake mixer

I can't imagine baking without an electric mixer. There are two types of electric mixers — stand mixers (21a) and portable electric hand-held mixers (21b). The hand-held mixer is very useful as it is affordable, and can be used when beating mixes over a double boiler. However, a hand-held mixer has a lower power level than a stand mixer, and it can get unique tiring to hold it constantly. Having both versions on hand would be ideal.

22 Silicone spatula

A silicone spatula is heatproof, which means you can use it to stir cake mixes as well as stir-fry ingredients. It is solid and long-lasting. I prefer using an integrated silicone spatula, which can be easily washed and kept clean, rather than a spatula with a wooden or plastic handle. A small spatula is also very useful in baking.

23 Pastry scraper

The humble pastry scraper is often referred to as a friend of the chef. This is a small but indispensable tool. I use it for cleaning floured tabletops, smoothing cookie dough, spreading sponge batter evenly in cake pans and scooping up cream. Choose a hard plastic scraper.

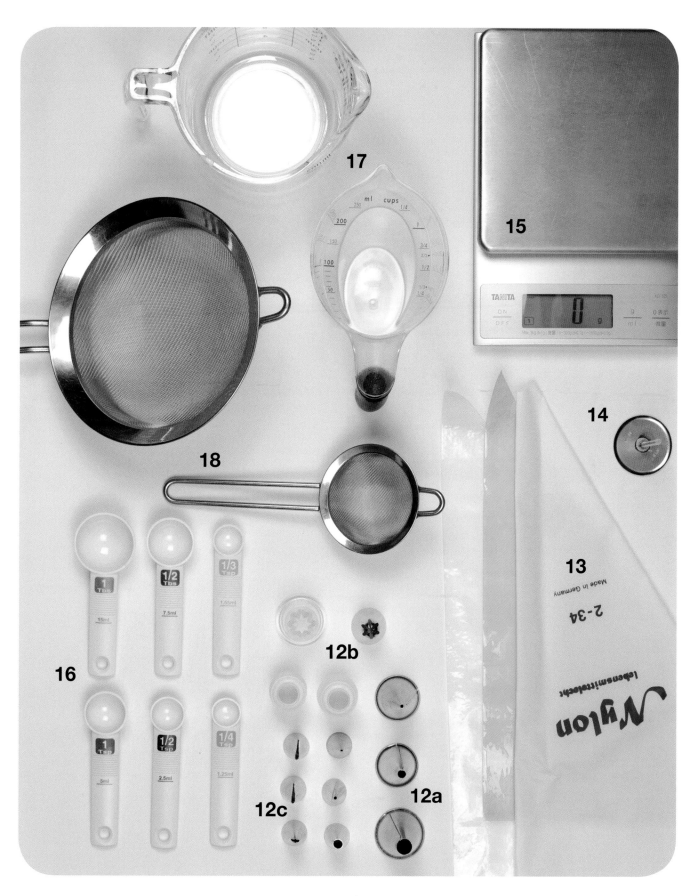

17

15

14

18

13
Made in Germany

2-34

Nylon
Lebensmittelecht

16

12b

12a

12c

24 Perforated wooden spatula

When cooking liquids such as custard sauce and jam, I prefer using a perforated wooden spatula with a straight edge. The holes of the spatula releases water pressure, which makes for easy stirring.

25 Food processer and stick blender

A food processer (25a) is useful for making dough for puff pastry and scones, as well as making cake mixtures and purées. A stick blender (25b) is used for processing small quantities of ingredients and for making purées.

26 Pastry brushes

A small brush (26a, about 2.5-cm width) is useful for buttering small cake pans and ramekins. A medium brush (26b, about 3-cm width) with natural soft bristles is handy for applying egg wash to cookies, pies and bread dough, and for brushing syrup on sponges and glazing jam on cakes. A big brush (26c, about 4-cm width) with natural bristles is useful for brushing excess flour from pieces of rolled-out dough.

27 Stainless steel or aluminium trays

Have these on hand to keep ingredients organised, to spread custard cream out for chilling or for placing under a cake rack when dusting with icing sugar or cocoa powder.

28 Rolling pin

Choose a wooden rolling pin that is slightly heavy. Its weight will help to flatten and push out dough while rolling it. A pin without a handle offers you the most control. My preference is for a 45-cm long and 3.5-cm diameter rolling pin.

29 Non-stick baking mat

Baking mats are heat-resistant, non-stick and reusable. A thin mat can be used in the same way as parchment paper. I use it to line the tart tin when blind-baking before adding aluminium weights. This helps ensure that the tart crust is kept even and flat.

21b

20

19

23

21a

22

24

30 Parchment paper and natural drawing paper

Parchment paper is used to line baking trays and cake pans. It is heat-resistant, non-stick and disposable. Natural drawing paper is the cheaper alternative to parchment paper, but it is not non-stick.

31 Saucepans and crepe pans

Use thick-based saucepans when cooking custard creams, sauces, syrups and jams. Saucepans that are at least 9-cm deep are ideal for stirring and mixing ingredients. When making crepes, use a heavy, thick-based pan. I use one that is 22 cm in diameter.

32 Citrus juicer

A citrus juicer makes juicing citrus fruit easy. Cut the fruit in half, then squeeze it on the sharp edge of the juicer to extract the juice.

33 Ruler

A ruler is useful when you have to cut cakes into equal layers and measure mould sizes.
I use a plastic ruler that can be easily washed and kept clean. A 40-cm ruler is adequate.

34 Grater

A grater can be used to grate the rind of citrus fruit like lemons and oranges. Do not grate the fruit too deeply, as the white part of the citrus fruit is bitter. Graters can also be used to grate hard ingredients such as hard cheese, chocolate and nutmeg.

35 Offset spatula and straight spatula

An offset spatula (35a) is a palette knife with an angled blade. A straight spatula (35b) is a palette knife with a long, flexible metal blade. These spatulas are used to spread and smoothen batter inside cake pans and spread cream evenly on cakes. It is useful to have the 26 cm and 18 cm straight spatulas, and 20 cm and 11 cm offset spatulas.

36 Serrated cake knife

A long knife (36a) is useful for slicing sponge cakes into layers without compressing it. A short knife (36b) is handy for cutting fruit, nuts, tarts and cakes.

25a

25b

30

27

32

26a 26b 26c

31 33 28 30 29

37 Dough thickness guides

This is a helpful tool for slicing cakes or rolling cookie dough into uniformly thick sheets. There are professional aluminium guides, but I use wooden sticks that I got from a DIY store. I have sticks that 3-mm, 5-mm, 10-mm and 15-mm thick.

38 Decorating turntable

This is useful for spreading the top and sides of cakes evenly with cream, and when applying decorations. A simple and small plastic turntable is good enough.

39 Digital kitchen timer

If your oven is not equipped with a timer, invest in a good digital timer to help you churn out perfectly baked cakes.

40 Cake tester and bamboo skewer

Test if a cake has been adequately baked by inserting a cake tester or bamboo skewer into the centre of the cake. The cake tester or bamboo skewer should come out clean.

41 Wire racks

Raised wire racks allow air to circulate around freshly baked cakes to cool them down. I find rectangular (28 × 43-cm) and round (30 cm diameter) wire racks most useful.

42 Blowtorch

A blowtorch is useful for unmoulding chilled cakes from cake moulds. It can also be used to caramelise Italian meringues and sugar on the surface of crème brûlées.

43 Electric ice cream maker

There are many types of ice cream makers available. When choosing one where the bowl needs to be chilled ahead of time, check that it will fit in your freezer.

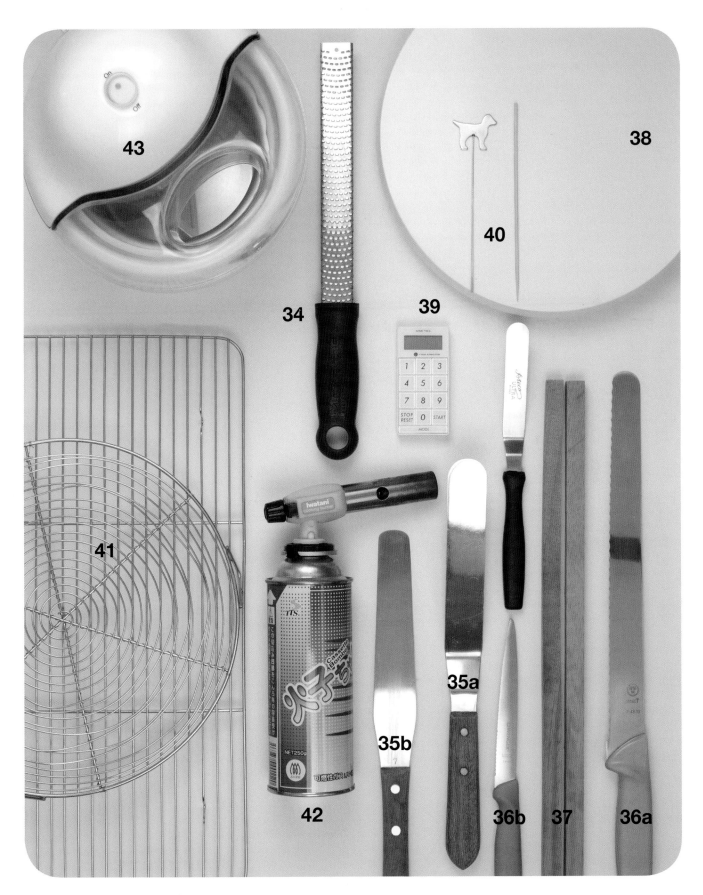

43

34

38

40

39

35a

35b

42

36b

37

36a

41

basic ingredients

EGGS

Eggs

In my recipes, I use whole eggs that weigh about 60 g. The weight of the egg white should be about 35 g and the yolk 15–20 g. It is best to choose the freshest eggs possible when baking. The eggs must also be at room temperature, so make sure to remove the eggs from the refrigerator about 30 minutes before you start baking. When separating egg yolks from egg whites, it is easier to use your hands instead of using the cracked shells, as the sharp edges of the shell may pierce the egg yolk. Egg whites can be frozen and kept in the freezer for up to one month.

WHEAT FLOURS

There are many varieties of white flour available and the names they go by may be different in different countries. White flour is made from the endosperm of wheat grains and there are two types of wheat: soft wheat and hard wheat. Soft wheat contains less protein than hard wheat, so white flour produced from the former contains less protein than the latter. White flour is classified by the amount of protein it contains. When the proteins in flour mixes with water, gluten is produced. This gluten gives the dough its elastic structure and taste, so different types of flour will produce baked goods with differing textures.

Cake flour

Cake flour is a low-gluten flour. It is made from soft wheat and contains 6–8 per cent protein. It is good for making sponge cakes, chiffon cakes and Swiss rolls.

Pastry flour

Pastry flour is also known as top four and is similar to cake flour. These types of flour contain 8–10 per cent protein and are suitable for making soft and light-textured cakes such as sponge and chiffon cakes, and lighter cookies and butter cakes. In France, flour that contains less than 9 per cent protein is called Type 45.

Plain flour

Plain flour is also known as all-purpose flour. It contains 9–11 per cent protein and is suitable for making puff pastry, cookies, butter cakes and pancakes and for using in cooking. In France, flour that contains 9–11 per cent protein is called Type 55.

Bread flour

Bread flour is a high-gluten flour. It contains 12–14 per cent protein which gives the baked product its shape and structure. High gluten flours are good for making bread.

STARCHES & LEAVENERS

Baking powder

Baking powder is a dry chemical leavening agent often used in baking. The most commonly used baking powder today is double-acting baking powder. Double-acting baking powder contains two acid salts: one which reacts at room temperature and the other which reacts at high temperature. If too much baking powder is added, it might leave a bitter aftertaste. Aluminium-free baking powder will not leave this aftertaste.

Cornflour

Cornflour is also known as cornstarch. It is milled from corn and is gluten-free. I often use it together with other types of flour to give my cakes a lighter texture. Cornflour is also used as a thickener in cooking.

Gelatin

Gelatin comes in two forms: powder and sheet. I prefer using gelatin sheets as it is more manageable. Gelatin is extracted from the collagen found inside an animal's skin and bones, and is made of protein. It melts when heated and solidifies when cool. Some fruit such as pineapple and kiwi contain an enzyme which breaks down protein, thus causing gelatin to lose its gelling abilities. I prefer using gelatin that absorbs 6 times its weight of water. Check the label on the packaging.

OILS

Unsalted butter

It is best to use unsalted butter when baking so as to control the amount of salt in the cake. The butter must be at room temperature for baking and not melted. Ideally, butter should be kept in the refrigerator in an airtight container because it tends to absorb odours quite easily. Butter can also be kept in the freezer for a longer period of time.

Canola oil, safflower oil and grape seed oil

These three types of oil are good for baking. They are relatively flavourless and are suitable for baking light cakes such as chiffon cakes. They also contain oleic acid, which is good for lowering cholesterol levels.

SWEETENERS

Castor (superfine) sugar

Castor sugar is a vital ingredient in baking. Made from cane sugar, the crystals are finer than regular white sugar and thus dissolves faster when mixed.

Light brown sugar and dark brown sugar

When you want to add more flavour and give some colour to your cakes, use brown and dark brown sugar. Although it is also made from cane sugar, brown sugar has more minerals than castor sugar, and it contains purified molasses.

Icing (confectioner's) sugar

Icing sugar is regular granulated sugar that is ground to a very fine powder. Some manufacturers add 1–2 per cent cornflour to help prevent the powdered sugar from clumping together due to humidity. The presence of cornflour in icing sugar renders it unsuitable for use in cold desserts such as jellies, as it affects appearance and taste. Read the label to check if cornflour has been added or if it is pure icing sugar. If using pure icing sugar, sift it before use.

Glucose

Glucose is a thick, clear syrup that is used in a variety of recipes to help cakes retain their moisture. It also controls the formation of sugar crystals. Light corn syrup and golden syrup are good substitutes for glucose.

Honey

Honey is another alternative sweetener to sugar. It helps cakes retain moisture while giving them a bouncy texture. The flavours and colours of honey varies according to the source of the nectar from which it is made. Acacia, clover, orange and lavender honey are suitable for use in baking.

Maple syrup

Maple syrup is made from the sap of sugar maple trees and is mainly produced in Canada. It is golden brown in colour and has a delicate flavour. Maple syrup is the preferred topping for pancakes, waffles and French toast. It can also be used in a variety of baked goods.

FLAVOURING AND COLOURING

Chocolate

There are so many varieties of chocolate available that you might find it rather difficult to choose a suitable chocolate for baking. My preference is for dark chocolate, coating dark and white chocolate and French cocoa powder. Dark chocolate is produced by adding cocoa butter and sugar to cocoa without the addition of milk. European standards specify that dark chocolate must contain a minimum of 35 per cent cocoa solids. Coating chocolate is useful for coating cakes and cookies. It contains cocoa powder, vegetable oil, sugar and milk powder, and doesn't require tempering. Cocoa powder is the non-fat part of cocoa bean, which is ground into a powder. It is unsweetened and very useful for baking. Store chocolate in a cool, dark and dry place.

Green tea powder

Green tea powder is made from green tea leaves, which are dried and ground into a fine powder. Traditionally used for brewing tea, green tea powder is now commonly used for flavouring pastries. Store in the freezer to prolong its shelf life.

Japanese pumpkin

Japanese pumpkin (*kabocha*) is smaller than the Western variety of pumpkin. It has dark green skin and orange flesh that is sweet with a firm texture, making it ideal for baking. Peel skin and remove the seeds before use.

Japanese red beans

Japanese red beans (*azuki*) are rich in protein and fibre. Red beans are regarded as a very nutritious food in Japanese cuisine. Although used in both savoury and sweet dishes, red beans are predominantly used in making Japanese-influenced Western pastries.

Liqueur

The addition of liqueur gives cakes a rich flavour, and I especially like using cherry, orange and rum in my recipes. When using liqueur in baking, I use drinking liqueur rather than those made for confectionery purposes as it has a richer flavour.

Vanilla

The vanilla bean is the second most expensive spice after saffron. With its complex floral aroma, it is an extremely popular and versatile spice. Madagascar produces high-grade vanilla beans which are often referred to as "Bourbon vanilla". Use this if available. Vanilla extract and vanilla paste are common substitutes. Vanilla beans can be frozen for better storage.

Spices

Dried spices as such ground ginger, ground allspice, ground cinnamon and cumin seeds are commonly used in baking, and give the baked products a strong flavour. Store dried spices in the freezer to prolong their shelf life.

Herbs

Dried and fresh herbs add flavour to baking. For fresh herbs, I like using rosemary and basil which I grow in my garden or from the supermarket. For dried herbs, I like using rose petals, peppermint, chamomile and lavender. I also use elder flower cordial and chicory powder. These ingredients can be purchased from herbal or health food shops, while peppermint and chamomile tea can be purchased from supermarkets.

Food colouring

I use food colouring to add colour to sugar icing and butter cream. Dip a toothpick into your preferred icing colour to add just a little to the mixture you want to colour. Repeat until you get the desired colour tone.

FRUIT, NUTS & SEEDS

Fresh fruit

I enjoy using a variety of fresh fruit such as strawberries, raspberries, oranges, lemons and yuzu in my baking. If using fruit such as strawberries for decorating cakes, choose smaller ones with a good rich colour.

Fruit purées

I often use fruit purées in baking as they are packed with flavour. In this book, I use frozen raspberry, strawberry and mango purées. Do note that some frozen purées contain about 10 per cent sugar. I typically buy a 1-kg pack of purée as it is more cost-effective, and divide it into 100-g portions before placing them in freezer bags in the freezer. I then thaw the amount as needed in the recipe.

Canned fruit and vegetables

Canned fruit are very useful in making cakes and desserts because they are readily available all year round. In these recipes, I use canned pear, yellow peach, Japanese white peach, Japanese grapes and red beets.

Dried fruit

These natural and tasty ingredients are very useful for baking. Some of my favourite dried fruit are Californian dried apricots, Turkish dried figs, dried cranberries, raisins and soft prunes.

Candied fruit

I also enjoy using candied fruit such as sliced candied orange peel in my baking. Candied orange peel is prepared by cooking the peel in thick sugar syrup, and can be kept for a long time. Candied cherries are lovely to use for Christmas cakes and cookies since they come in festive red and green colours.

Chestnuts

I use chestnut paste and steamed chestnuts in this book. Do note that chestnut paste and chestnut spread are different products although they are both sold canned. Chestnut spread is similar to jam while chestnut paste is thicker and more like a solid. Steamed chestnuts are sold in snack packs in the supermarket.

Almonds

The almond is a versatile nut that can be used in many ways. Spanish and Californian almonds are popularly used in baking. They come in different forms, including whole, sliced, slivered, diced and ground. Whole almonds are usually blanched and shelled. Toasting them lightly before use brings out their flavour. Almonds are best kept in the freezer to ensure freshness.

Walnuts

Shelled walnuts are used in many recipes. Californian and Chinese walnuts are popular, although I prefer Californian walnuts as Chinese ones tend to have a bitter taste. Toasting them lightly before use brings out their flavour. Walnuts must be kept dry and preferably refrigerated. I always keep them in the freezer as they oxidise easily.

Pecans

Pecans taste similar to walnuts, but have a less bitter taste. Pecans are another popular nut used in baking.

Black and white sesame seeds

Sesame seeds have a strong nutty flavour and aroma which is brought out when toasted. Sesame seeds can be used whole or ground in baking. As they have a high oil content, keep refrigerated to extend their shelf-life.

SOY, DAIRY & COCONUT PRODUCTS

Soy bean powder and soy bean milk

Soy bean powder (*kinako*) has a fragrant, nutty flavour and is popularly used in many Japanese sweets. Soy milk has about the same amount of protein as cow's milk. It is rich in vitamins B and E and has no cholesterol. Soy milk is a good substitute for cow's milk, and is a vegetarian option.

Cream cheese

Cream cheese is commonly used to make cheesecakes. I prefer using French cream cheese to American cream cheese as it is less salty and has a softer texture.

Whipping cream

There are several types of whipping cream, and they sometimes go by different names. Choose the right whipping cream according to the fat content labelled on the packet. Depending on the recipe, I use French whipping cream, which contains around 35 per cent fat and Australian thickened cream, which contains around 45 per cent fat.

Milk

I use fresh whole milk when baking as it has a richer, fresher taste than low fat and UHT milk. Substitute as necessary according to your dietary requirements and preferences.

Coconut

In this book, I use dried grated coconut, coconut cream powder and coconut cream, all of which give a rich coconut flavour to baking. Do note that coconut cream is different from coconut milk. Coconut cream is thick and creamy with a strong flavour.

new creations
(western pastries with a japanese touch)

green tea soufflé cheesecake

Makes one 18-cm round cake

Pastry flour 45 g, sifted twice

Green tea powder 5 g, sifted twice

Eggs 3

Castor sugar 70 g

GREEN TEA CREAM CHEESE LAYER

Cream cheese 150 g

Castor sugar 65 g

Pastry flour 25 g, sifted

Green tea powder 7 g, sifted

Egg yolks 3

Fresh whole milk 180 g

Whipping cream (35% fat) 80 g

MERINGUE

Egg whites 2

Castor sugar 40 g

NOTE: Do not overbeat the meringue as it might cause the cake to shrink.

To make a plain soufflé cheese cake, replace the green tea powder with 2 tsp lemon juice and add after the cream cheese mixture is thickened.

1. Preheat oven to 200°C. Line a shallow 28-cm square cake pan with parchment paper.

2. Sift pastry flour and green tea powder together twice. Set aside. Beat eggs lightly using an electric mixer. Add sugar and beat at high speed until light and fluffy. Reduce speed to low and continue beating for about 1 minute. Add green tea flour mixture and gently fold in with a spatula.

3. Pour batter into prepared cake pan and spread evenly with a scraper. Place cake pan on a baking tray and bake for 10–12 minutes. When sponge is done, remove from pan and place in a big plastic bag to cool.

4. Line an 18-cm round cake pan with parchment paper. Peel brown skin from cooled sponge and cut out an 18-cm round. Place into round cake pan.

5. Preheat oven to 160°C.

6. Make green tea cream cheese layer. Microwave cream cheese at 600 w for 30 seconds or until softened. Place sugar, flour and green tea powder in a bowl and mix well. Add cream cheese and egg yolks and mix well.

7. Make meringue. Beat egg whites in a clean bowl until foamy. Add half the sugar and continue beating for 1 minute. Add remaining sugar and beat until stiff peaks form and meringue is glossy. Set aside.

8. Heat milk and whipping cream in a small saucepan. Remove from heat just before it comes to a boil. Add to cream cheese mixture and mix well. Return mixture to the saucepan and bring to a boil over low heat. When mixture thickens a little, remove from heat.

9. Beat meringue again until glossy, then mix well with cream cheese mixture using a whisk. Pour into prepared round cake pan.

10. Place on a baking tray and add enough hot water to come halfway up the side of pan. Bake for 1 hour 10 minutes.

11. Place cake on a wire rack to cool before removing from pan. Chill in the refrigerator before slicing to serve.

polka-dotted green tea roll cake

Makes one 28-cm roll cake

Egg whites 140 g

Castor sugar 90 g

Egg yolks 5

Pastry flour 55 g, sifted twice

Unsalted butter 40 g, melted

Green tea powder 2 g

GREEN TEA CREAM

Whipping cream (35% fat) 150 g

Green tea powder 6 g

Castor sugar 20 g

Gelatin sheets 3 g, soaked in
   iced water to soften

Fresh whole milk ½ Tbsp

Home-made red bean paste
   150 g (page 48)

NOTE: To make a plain roll cake,
omit the green tea powder.

1. Preheat oven to 200°C. Line a shallow 28-cm square cake pan with parchment paper.

2. Place egg whites in a clean bowl and beat until foamy. Add one-third of sugar and continue beating for a few minutes, then add remaining sugar and beat until stiff peaks form and meringue is glossy.

3. Add egg yolks and fold in lightly. Add flour and fold gently with a spatula. Add hot melted butter and fold through.

4. Take 40 g of mixture and add green tea powder to it. Mix well and spoon into a small disposable piping bag (or plastic bag). Cut a small hole at the tip. Pipe several small circles on prepared cake pan.

5. Pour batter gently over circles and spread carefully with a scraper. Place cake pan on a tray and bake for 10–13 minutes. Remove cake from pan and place in a big plastic bag to cool.

6. Make green tea cream. Place cream, green tea powder and castor sugar in a clean bowl, then place bowl over another bowl filled with ice cubes and water. Using an electric mixer, whisk at medium speed until stiff peaks form and cream is smooth. Do not ovebeat. Place softened gelatin and milk in a small bowl set over a double boiler to melt gelatin. Add melted gelatin and milk mixture to green tea cream and mix quickly.

7. Turn cooled sponge onto a clean work surface. Peel off parchment paper from bottom of sponge. Spread an even layer of green tea cream over sponge. Spoon red bean paste in a line across one end of sponge, then gently roll sponge up. Cover with parchment paper, then chill in the freezer for a short while to set. Slice into even pieces and serve.

pumpkin cake

Makes one 20-cm Bundt cake

Unsalted butter 110 g,
   at room temperature

Pastry flour 240 g

Baking powder 4 tsp

Japanese pumpkin, skinned 200 g

Japanese pumpkin (with skin) 100 g,
   cut into small pieces, some reserved
   for topping

Brown sugar 200 g

Salt a pinch

Eggs 100 g, about 2 eggs

Fresh whole milk 80 g

Ground cinnamon 1$^{1}/_{2}$ tsp

Walnuts 80 g, chopped and
   baked for 20 minutes at 160°C,
   20 g reserved for topping

Raisins 60 g, soaked overnight in rum,
   some reserved for topping

Apricot jam 100 g

Pumpkin seeds $^{1}/_{2}$ Tbsp

NOTE: I used Japanese pumpkin in this recipe
as it has less moisture than other types of
pumpkin. If Japanese pumpkin is not available,
choose a pumpkin that is not watery.

1. Lightly grease a 20-cm Bundt pan with softened butter. Place in the freezer
    to chill. Dust pan with flour, then overturn pan to remove any excess flour.
    Line 2–3 muffin cups with paper cases to bake any extra batter.

2. Sift flour and baking powder together twice.

3. Microwave skinned pumpkin at 600 w for about 3 minutes until soft,
    and pumpkin with skin for about 1$^{1}/_{2}$ minutes. Purée skinned pumpkin
    in a food processer. Set aside.

4. Preheat oven to 170°C.

5. Place butter, brown sugar and salt in a bowl, and beat until creamy.
    Add eggs slowly, followed by pumpkin purée and mix well.

6. Add half the flour mixture and mix with a whisk. Add milk and mix batter
    gently. Add remaining flour mixture, walnuts, raisins and pumpkin with skin,
    and fold through.

7. Pour batter into prepared Bundt pan and any excess batter into muffin cups.

8. Bake for 35–45 minutes or until cake has a springy texture when pressed
    gently. The muffins will bake faster.

9. When the cake is done, remove from pan and place on a wire rack until cool.

10. Microwave apricot jam at 600 w for 30 seconds, then brush evenly over
    cake. Top with pumpkin, walnuts, raisins and pumpkin seeds.

green tea pound cake

Makes one 24 x 8-cm cake

Pastry flour 110 g

Baking powder ¹/₂ tsp

Green tea powder 10 g

Unsalted butter 120 g,
   at room temperature

Icing sugar 120 g

Salt a pinch

Eggs 120 g

Japanese chestnuts in syrup
   (*kanro-ni*) about 15 pieces +
   more for topping

GREEN TEA ICING

Icing sugar 160 g

Green tea powder 5 g

Water 2 Tbsp

NOTE: For a different flavour, omit the chestnuts or replace with red bean paste.

By making a 'cut' in the middle of the batter, the pound cake will develop a clean, straight crack after baking.

1. Preheat oven to 170°C. Line a 24 x 8 x 6-cm cake pan with parchment paper.

2. Sift flour, baking powder and green tea powder together twice.

3. Beat butter, icing sugar and salt until light and very fluffy. Gradually add eggs and beat well. Add flour mixture and fold through completely using a spatula. The surface of batter should be glossy and smooth.

4. Pour half the batter into prepared cake pan, then arrange chestnuts in a line in the middle. Pour remaining batter over to cover chestnuts, and make a lengthwise 'cut' down the middle with a spatula. Bake for about 50 minutes.

5. Remove cake from pan and place in a big plastic bag to cool.

6. Make green tea icing. Place icing sugar and green tea powder in a small bowl and mix well. Add water and mix until smooth.

7. Pour green tea icing over cake. Decorate with gold dust and chopped chestnuts, if desired.

yuzu chiffon cake

Makes one 20-cm cake

Egg yolks 5

Castor sugar 20 g

Yuzu 2, about 300 g, rind finely grated
and fruit squeezed to extract 60 g juice
(top up with water if necessary)

Pastry flour 80 g, sifted twice

Vegetable oil 60 g

Whipping cream (35% fat) 200 g

**Yuzu jam (store-bought
or home-made)** 60 g

MERINGUE

Castor sugar 90 g

Cornflour 10 g

Egg whites 180 g, about 5 eggs

YUZU JAM (OPTIONAL)

Yuzu 2, about 300 g

Castor sugar 210 g or 70% of
yuzu weight

Water 100 g

1. Preheat oven to 160°C. Prepare a 20-cm chiffon cake tube pan.

2. Combine egg yolks and sugar in a bowl and mix well. Add yuzu juice and oil and blend together. Add flour and mix until batter becomes sticky. Set aside.

3. Make meringue. Combine sugar and cornflour. Beat egg whites until foamy. Add half the sugar mixture and continue beating for a few minutes, then add remaining sugar mixture and beat until stiff peaks form and meringue is glossy.

4. Add one-third of meringue to egg yolk mixture and fold in lightly, then add remaining meringue and fold to incorporate completely.

5. Pour batter into ungreased chiffon cake tube pan. Bake for 40–50 minutes. Remove cake from oven and overturn pan. Leave until cake is cool.

6. Make whipped cream. Place whipping cream in a clean bowl, then place bowl over another bowl filled with ice cubes and water. Using an electric mixer, whisk at medium speed until stiff peaks form and cream is smooth. Do not overbeat or cream will become grainy.

7. Serve cake with whipped cream and store-bought or home-made yuzu jam.

8. To make yuzu jam, cut yuzu in half. Squeeze for juice and remove rind and segments. Weigh juice, segments and rind, and weigh sugar to make up 70% weight of yuzu. Chop segments finely and slice rind thinly. Place rind in a saucepan and add water to cover rind. Bring to a boil, then strain rind. Place yuzu juice, segments and rind with sugar and 100 g water in a saucepan. Bring to a boil, skimming off any scum that floats to the surface. Simmer for about 15 minutes over low heat, stirring occasionally. Let cool before serving. To store, pour hot jam into sterilised jam jars and seal tightly.

mille crepe with black sesame cream

Makes one 18-cm round cake

Pastry flour 110 g

Cornflour 40 g

Eggs 3

Castor sugar 75 g

Fresh whole milk 350 g

Unsalted butter 40 g, melted

BLACK SESAME CREAM

Pastry flour 10 g

Cornflour 10 g

Fresh whole milk 200 g

Egg yolks 3

Castor sugar 50 g

Black sesame paste 60 g

WHIPPED CREAM

Whipping cream (35% fat) 200 g

Castor sugar 1 Tbsp

NOTE: Instead of making a mille crepe, you can also enjoy the crepes on their own using this recipe. Serve crepes with salted butter and sugar.

1. Sift flour and cornflour together. Beat eggs and sugar with a whisk. Add flour mixture and mix well. Add milk gradually until just combined. Add melted butter and mix well. Let mixture sit for about 30 minutes.

2. Make black sesame cream. Sift flour and cornflour together twice. Add milk to a saucepan and bring to a boil. In a clean bowl, beat egg yolks and sugar together until mixture is pale yellow. Add flour mixture and mix well. Add hot milk and fold through. Return egg and milk mixture to saucepan and bring to a boil over high heat, stirring constantly with a whisk. Continue mixing until mixture is smooth and glossy, then remove saucepan from heat.

3. Transfer pastry cream to a tray, cover with cling film and place in the freezer to cool. Do not freeze it. Before using, gently beat cream and black sesame paste with an electric mixer until smooth and creamy.

4. Make crepes. Place a crepe pan over low heat and grease lightly with butter. Spread 2 Tbsp crepe mixture thinly over pan and cook for 10–15 seconds until crepe is golden. Flip crepe over and cook for a few seconds. Remove from pan. Repeat to make 15 crepes. Set aside.

5. Make whipped cream. Place whipping cream and sugar in a clean bowl, then place bowl over another bowl filled with ice cubes and water. Using an electric mixer, whisk at medium speed until stiff peaks form and cream is smooth.

6. Place a crepe on a plate and spread with a thin layer of black sesame cream. Top with a second crepe and spread with a thin layer of whipped cream. Repeat to layer until crepes are used up.

7. Slice and serve immediately.

green tea/black sesame scones

Makes 10–12 scones

GREEN TEA/BLACK SESAME SCONES

Unsalted butter 80 g, cut into small cubes

Pastry flour 220 g

Baking powder 1 Tbsp

Castor sugar 60 g (reduce to 40 g
  for black sesame scones)

Salt 1/8 tsp

Green tea powder 12 g OR
  Black sesame paste 50 g

Fresh whole milk 120 g, cold +
  more for brushing

WHIPPED CREAM

Whipping cream (35% fat) 200 g

Castor sugar 1 Tbsp

RED BEAN PASTE (OPTIONAL)

Red beans (adzuki) 500 g, rinsed

Castor sugar 430 g

Salt 1/2 tsp

NOTE: For plain scones, use 30 g castor sugar
and 110 g egg yolk and milk mixture that is a
combination of 1 egg yolk with enough fresh
whole milk to make up amount.

1. Place butter, flour, baking powder, sugar, salt and green pea powder in a plastic bag and refrigerate overnight. For black sesame scones, omit green tea powder.

2. Preheat oven to 200°C. Line a baking tray with parchment paper.

3. Pulse chilled ingredients in a food processor until mixture resembles coarse breadcrumbs. Transfer to a bowl and add cold milk and black sesame paste if making black sesame scones. Fold with a scraper until dough is formed.

4. Place dough on a floured surface and knead lightly. Roll out to a thickness of about 2 cm. Dust a 4.5-cm round cutter with flour and cut out as many rounds of dough as possible. Place on baking tray and brush with milk.

5. Bake for 12–15 minutes until scones are golden brown. Remove from heat and cool on a wire rack.

6. Make whipped cream. Place whipping cream and sugar in a clean bowl, then place bowl over another bowl filled with ice cubes and water. Using an electric mixer, whisk at medium speed until soft peaks form.

7. Serve scones warm with whipped cream and store-bought or home-made red bean paste on the side.

8. To make red bean paste, bring red beans to a boil in a pot of water. Drain and transfer beans to a saucepan. Add enough water to cover beans and simmer over low heat for about 2 hours until beans are soft. Skim off any foam. Pour beans into a cloth and return to saucepan. Add sugar and cook over low heat, stirring constantly for 7–10 minutes. Add salt and mix well. Leave to cool. Paste can be stored for up to 1 week in an airtight container in the refrigerator, or up to 2 months in the freezer.

red bean coconut pie

Makes one 22-cm round pie

Home-made red bean paste
  250 g (page 48)

Apricot jam 70 g

SHORTCRUST PASTRY

Unsalted butter 60 g,
  cut into small cubes

Pastry flour 100 g

Castor sugar ¼ tsp

Salt ⅛ tsp

Ice-cold water 50 g

COCONUT TOPPING

Sour cream 130 g

Castor sugar 30 g

Vanilla extract ½ tsp

Desiccated coconut 60 g

Egg 1, about 50 g

NOTE: For a different flavour, replace the red bean paste with sliced bananas. Place the sliced bananas on the baked tart shell and pour the coconut topping over. Spread the topping out evenly, then bake as for red bean coconut pie.

1. Make shortcrust pastry. Combine butter, flour, sugar and salt in a plastic bag and place in the freezer overnight. Using a food processor, pulse chilled ingredients until mixture resembles coarse breadcrumbs. Add water and mix until dough is formed. Place dough on a floured surface and knead lightly. Put dough into a plastic bag and refrigerate overnight.

2. Preheat oven 200°C. Prepare a 22-cm fluted tart tin with a removable base.

3. Place dough on a floured work surface and roll out to a thickness of about 5 mm. Brush away excess flour and place dough over tart tin. Gently press dough into side and bottom edges of tin. Roll a rolling pin over top of tin to trim edges. Prick dough with a fork and let rest for 5 minutes in the freezer.

4. Place a sheet of aluminum foil or a non-stick mat over chilled dough (without covering edges of dough), and press it well into the bottom edges. Place baking weights into tart tin and bake for 20 minutes. Remove weights and aluminium foil when pastry just begins to colour around the edges and continue baking for another 10 minutes until light golden brown. Remove from heat and leave to cool on a wire rack.

5. Preheat oven to 180°C.

6. Make coconut topping. Place sour cream, sugar and vanilla in a bowl and mix well. Add desiccated coconut and egg and mix well.

7. Spread red bean paste on prepared tart shell, then top with coconut topping. Use an offset spatula to spread topping out evenly. Bake for 30–40 minutes or until topping is golden brown. Set aside to cool.

8. Microwave apricot jam at 600 w for 30 seconds and brush over pie. Slice and serve.

black sesame soy bean pudding

Makes 5 servings

Gelatin sheets 5 g

White sesame seeds 70 g

Soy bean milk 330 g

Castor sugar 40 g

Whipping cream (35% fat) 200 g

BLACK SUGAR SYRUP

Black sugar 50 g

Water 50 g

NOTE: This recipe makes five small portions. Double the recipe if needed. Soy bean milk can also be replaced with fresh whole milk.

1. Prepare five 90-ml wine glasses. Soak gelatin sheets in iced water to soften.

2. Bake white sesame seeds for about 15 minutes at 160°C without preheating oven. Grind toasted white sesame seeds in a food processer.

3. Place ground white sesame seeds, soy bean milk and sugar in a saucepan and bring to a boil. Turn off heat, cover pan and let sit for about 10 minutes for flavours to infuse.

4. Strain soy milk through a sieve into a bowl, pressing white sesame seeds lightly to release excess liquid. Weigh liquid. It should be about 250 g. If weight is below 250 g, add more soy bean milk to make up 250 g. If it is more than 250 g, remove excess liquid.

5. Place softened gelatin in a bowl and heat gently in a double boiler until melted. Add melted gelatin and whipping cream to soymilk and stir until gelatin is dissolved. Pour into wine glasses. Refrigerate overnight to set and chill.

6. Make black sugar syrup. Place black sugar and water into a small saucepan and simmer for about 8 minutes, stirring until syrup is a little thick. Skim off any scum occasionally. Leave to cool.

7. Pour black sugar syrup on set pudding and serve.

black sugar crème caramel

Makes 7 servings

Castor sugar 100 g

Hot water 40 g

Fresh whole milk 500 g

Black sugar 90 g

Vanilla extract 1 tsp

Eggs 3

Egg yolks 3

NOTE: To make plain crème caramel, replace black sugar with castor sugar and use a vanilla bean instead of vanilla extract. Split the pod lengthwise, scrape the seeds and add both pod and seeds to the milk. Remove the pod before adding the egg mixture.

1. Preheat oven to 160°C. Prepare 7 small 7.5-cm muffin cups or 8.5-cm ramekins.

2. Make caramel. Place castor sugar in a saucepan over medium heat and stir with a spatula until sugar is melted. Continue to heat until sugar is caramelised. Add hot water and mix well. (Be careful not to be scalded by the hot steam.) Immediately pour caramel equally into muffin cups or ramekins and place into the freezer to set.

3. Place milk, black sugar and vanilla in a saucepan. Leave to sit for about 10 minutes, then heat until mixture is just below the boiling point. Remove from heat.

4. In a mixing bowl, beat eggs and egg yolks lightly. Pour warm milk mixture into egg mixture and mix well.

5. Place chilled muffin cups or ramekins in a deep baking tray, and pour egg and milk mixture equally over caramel.

6. Fill baking tray with enough hot water to come halfway up the sides of cups or ramekins. Bake for 40–45 minutes or until custard is set. Remove cups or ramekins from tray and refrigerate until cold.

7. To unmould, dip base of each cup or ramekin into hot water for 5 seconds, then press edge of custard and invert crème caramel onto a serving plate. Serve immediately.

kinako shortbread

Makes about 30 cookies

 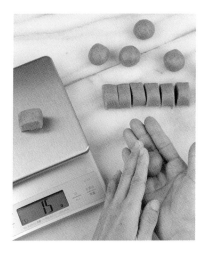 

Pastry flour 140 g

Rice flour 40 g

Soy bean powder (*kinako*) 50 g

Baking powder 1/2 tsp

Unsalted butter 140 g,
    at room temperature

Castor sugar 50 g + more for sprinkling

NOTE: To make plain shortbread, replace flour mixture with 180 g pastry flour and 30 g rice flour, and add 1 tsp vanilla extract.

1. Line a baking tray with parchment paper. Sift pastry flour, rice flour, soy bean powder and baking powder together twice.

2. Preheat oven to 160°C.

3. Beat butter and sugar until softened. Add flour mixture and mix with a spatula or scraper until a smooth dough forms. If dough becomes sticky and is difficult to handle, place in the refrigerator to chill until it is no longer sticky.

4. Roll dough into a cylinder and cut to get 30 pieces, each weighing about 20 g. Roll each piece into a ball and place on prepared baking tray.

5. Flatten dough by pressing your thumb into the centre of each ball, then use a bamboo skewer to prick each disc. Sprinkle with sugar.

6. Bake for 20–25 minutes. Remove from heat and place shortbread on a wire rack to cool.

7. Store in an airtight container with a desiccant. Shortbread will for up to 2 weeks.

green tea cross cookies

Makes about 70 cookies

GREEN TEA DOUGH

Pastry flour 400 g

Green tea powder 20 g

Unsalted butter 270 g,
at room temperature

Icing sugar 140 g

Egg yolks 3

Salt a pinch

PLAIN DOUGH

Pastry flour 270 g, sifted

Salt a pinch

Unsalted butter 180 g,
at room temperature

Icing sugar 90 g

Egg yolks 2

NOTE: Besides a cross, you can vary the design to make chequerboard or stripe cookies.

The green tea powder can be replaced with 35 g cocoa powder to make chocolate cookies.

Any excess dough can be used to make marble cookies. Combine excess green tea and plain dough, and shape into a 4-cm diameter log. Wrap log with cling film and freeze overnight. Slice and bake as instructed in recipe.

1. Make green tea dough. Sift flour and green tea powder together twice. Beat butter and icing sugar until softened, then add egg yolks and mix well. Add green tea flour mixture and fold with a spatula or a scraper until a smooth dough forms.

2. Take 400 g of green tea dough and divide into 2. Place one portion on a non-stick baking mat. Cover surface with cling film and roll out into a 26 × 16-cm rectangular sheet, 3-mm thick. Repeat with other half of dough. Roll remaining green tea dough into a 26 x 14-cm sheet, 1-cm thick. Wrap and chill in the freezer for about 30 minutes. Set excess dough aside (see Note).

3. Repeat step 1 to make plain dough. Omit green tea powder and add salt. Roll plain dough into a 26 x 12-cm rectangular sheet, 1-cm thick. Wrap and chill in the freezer for about 30 minutes. Set excess dough aside (see Note).

4. Cut 10 bars, each 26 x 1-cm from 26 x 14-cm green tea sheet. Cut 8 bars, each 26 x 1-cm from plain sheet. Brush bars with water and arrange to form a cross. Make 2 logs.

5. Brush a 26 x 16-cm green tea rectangle with water and place a log on it. Wrap log tightly. Repeat to wrap other log. Using cling flim, wrap both logs and freeze overnight.

6. Preheat oven to 160°C. Slice logs into 7-mm thick pieces and roll edges in granulated sugar. Place on a lined baking tray and bake for about 25 minutes. Remove from heat and place on a wire rack to cool.

7. Store cookies in an airtight container with a dessicant. Cookies will keep for up to 2 weeks.

galette nantaise kinako

Makes about 30 cookies

Pastry flour 150 g

Soy bean powder (*kinako*) 50 g

Icing sugar 40 g +50 g

Ground almonds 70 g

Egg whites 12 g

Unsalted butter 150 g,
   at room temperature

Salt a pinch

EGG WASH

Egg yolk 1

Water ¹/₂ tsp

NOTE: To make plain galettes, replace
soy bean powder with an additional 50 g
pastry flour and 1 tsp vanilla extract.

1. Sift pastry flour and soy bean powder together twice.

2. Place 40 g icing sugar, ground almonds and egg whites into a food processor and blend well. Add butter gradually and blend well. Add remaining 50 g icing sugar and salt. Blend well, then add flour mixture and blend again.

3. Place dough on a non-stick baking mat. Cover surface with cling film or another baking mat and roll out to a thickness of about 5 mm. Transfer dough sheet with baking mat to a tray and place in the freezer for 20 minutes, so dough will be easier to handle.

4. Preheat oven 160°C. Line a baking tray with parchment paper.

5. Remove chilled dough from freezer and peel away cling film or baking mat covering the top of dough. Use a 6.5-cm fluted round cutter to cut out as many rounds as you can from dough. Arrange on prepared baking tray.

6. Make egg wash by mixing egg yolk with water in a small bowl. Brush egg wash on surface of galettes, then score using a fork.

7. Bake for 20–25 minutes. Remove from heat and place galettes on a wire rack to cool.

8. Store in an airtight container with a desiccant. Galettes will for up to 2 weeks.

all-time favourites

prune clafoutis
Makes 4–5 servings

Softened butter, for greasing

Soft prunes 15

Pastry flour 30 g

Cornflour 10 g

Castor sugar 90 g

Eggs 2

Egg yolk 1

Fresh whole milk 150 g

Whipping cream (35% fat) 100 g

Vanilla extract 1 tsp

NOTE: Clafoutis is a traditional French dessert originating from Limousin in central France. It was originally made using black cherries, the special produce of this district. Clafoutis tastes like custard pudding and has a texture like crepes.

1. Preheat oven to 180°C. Grease a 22-cm ovenproof dish with softened butter and set aside. If the prunes are very dry, place them in a pot of boiling water briefly, then strain and pat dry using paper towels. Set aside.

2. Make batter. Combine pastry flour, cornflour and castor sugar in a bowl and mix well. Add eggs and egg yolk and mix until no trace of flour is seen. Add milk, whipping cream and vanilla and mix well.

3. Spread prunes out on prepared ovenproof dish, then pour batter over.

4. Bake for 30–40 minutes, until surface of clafoutis is browned and centre springs back when touched.

5. Remove from heat and leave clafoutis to cool on a wire rack.

6. The clafoutis can be enjoyed warm, at room temperature or chilled. Dust with icing sugar before serving.

dome-shaped peach cake

Makes one 15-cm round cake

Canned Japanese white peach 4 halves

Pastry flour 90 g

Eggs 135 g

Egg yolk 1

Castor sugar 90 g

Unsalted butter 20 g

Fresh whole milk 20 g

Vanilla extract 1/2 tsp

JELLY

Canned peach syrup (from can) 300 g

Lemon juice 2 tsp

Gelatin sheets 10 g, soaked in iced water
  to soften

Red food colouring a drop

SUGAR SYRUP

Water 30 g

Castor sugar 15 g

Kirsch (cherry liqueur) 1 Tbsp

WHIPPED CREAM

Whipping cream (35% fat) 300 g

Castor sugar 20 g

Kirsch (cherry liqueur) 2 tsp

1. Drain canned peaches and reserve syrup. Slice half a peach half very thinly to decorate top of cake. Pat dry and set aside. Slice remaining peaches thinly and set aside.

2. Make jelly. Combine peach syrup and lemon juice in a bowl. Place softened gelatin in a small bowl and melt over a double boiler. Add to peach syrup. Stir in food colouring and mix well. Pour mixture into a container and refrigerate until set. Mince jelly and keep refrigerated until needed.

3. Preheat oven to 160°C. Prepare a 15-cm round cake pan with removable base. Line with parchment paper.

4. Sift flour twice. Set aside. In a mixing bowl, beat eggs and egg yolk with an electric whisk, then add sugar. Place bowl over a double boiler and beat well. When egg mixture is warm, beat at high speed until light and fluffy. Reduce speed to low and continue beating for about 1 minute. Gently fold in flour with a spatula.

5. Combine butter, milk and vanilla in a bowl and place over a double boiler. Stir until butter is melted. Add one-fifth of egg batter to butter mixture and mix well, then add to rest of egg batter and fold through evenly.

6. Pour batter into prepared cake pan and bake for 45–50 minutes or until cake springs back when touched. Remove from pan and place on a wire rack in a big plastic bag to cool. When cooled, trim crust off the top and bottom, then slice cake horizontally to make 3 layers, each about 1.3-cm.

7. Make sugar syrup. Combine water, sugar and chery liqueur in a bowl and mix well. Brush cakes evenly with sugar syrup.

8. Make whipped cream. Combine whipping cream, sugar and chery liqueur in a clean bowl. Place bowl over another bowl filled with ice cubes and water. Using an electric mixer, whisk cream at medium speed until stiff peaks form and cream is smooth.

9. Place a layer of cake on a flat tray. Spread with whipped cream, then top with a layer of sliced peaches and cover with cream. Repeat layering, then cover with third layer of cake. Cover with cling wrap and press cake down on the sides to create a dome shape. Chill in the freezer for a few minutes to set.

10. Unwrap cake and spread with remaining whipped cream. Decorate with thinly sliced peaches and minced jelly. Slice and serve immediately.

strawberry mousse charlotte cake

Makes one 18-cm round cake

Fresh strawberries and raspberries

STRAWBERRY JELLY

Strawberry purée 130 g

Castor sugar 40 g

Gelatin sheets 5 g, soaked in
iced water to soften

BISCUIT SPONGE

Pastry flour 60 g

Eggs 2

Castor sugar 60 g

Vanilla extract 1 tsp

STRAWBERRY MOUSSE

Strawberry purée 230 g

Castor sugar 100 g

Lemon juice 1 Tbsp

Gelatin sheets 10 g, soaked in iced water
to soften

Whipping cream (35% fat) 200 g

Kirsch (cherry liqueur) ¹/₂ Tbsp

1. Prepare strawberry jelly a day in advance. Mix strawberry purée and
sugar in a bowl until sugar is dissolved. Place softened gelatin in a small
bowl and melt over a double boiler. Add to strawberry mixture and mix well.
Wrap a 15-cm cake ring with cling wrap and place on a tray. Pour
strawberry mixture into cake ring and freeze overnight to set.

2. Preheat oven to 200°C. Line a baking pan with parchment paper.

3. Make biscuit sponge. Sift flour twice. Separate egg whites and yolks.
Beat yolks lightly and add half the sugar and vanilla. Whisk until mixture
thickens and becomes pale. Set aside.

4. Make meringue. Place egg whites in a clean bowl and beat until foamy.
Add remaining sugar and beat until stiff peaks form and meringue is glossy.
Add one-third of meringue to egg yolk mixture and fold lightly. Add flour
and fold well. Add remaining meringue and fold until just incorporated.

5. Fit a piping bag with a 1-cm round piping tip. Fill bag with batter and pipe
diagonal lines to form a 35 ×10-cm sheet and pipe a 16-cm disc on
prepared baking tray. Dust icing sugar over rectangular batter twice. Bake
for 10 minutes. Remove cake from tray and place on a wire rack to cool.
Once cooled, carefully peel parchment from biscuit. Cut out two 32 × 3.5-cm
bands from rectangular sheet.

6. Make sugar syrup. Combine water, sugar and kirsch in a bowl and mix well.

7. Line a tray with cling wrap and place an 18-cm cake ring on it. Fit an 18-cm
round cakeboard into cake ring. Place 2 bands of biscuit along the side of
ring, and 16-cm biscuit disc at the bottom. Brush disc lightly with sugar syrup.

WHIPPED CREAM
Whipping cream (35% fat) 100 g

Castor sugar 2 tsp

SUGAR SYRUP
Water 20 g

Castor sugar 10 g

Kirsch (cherry liqueur) ¹/₂ tsp

NOTE: Charlotte cake is a traditional French confection and charlotte is the French term for a lady's frilly hat. To vary this recipe, you can replace strawberry mousse with any fruit flavour mousse. The mousse can also be set in a glass bowl or in glasses and served as dessert.

8. Make strawberry mousse. Place strawberry purée, sugar and lemon juice in a bowl, and mix well until sugar is dissolved. Put softened gelatin in a small bowl and melt over a double boiler. Add to strawberry mixture and mix well. Place whipping cream in a clean bowl, then place bowl over another bowl filled with ice cubes and water. Using an electric mixer, whisk cream at medium speed until soft peaks form. Add whipped cream to strawberry mixture and mix well. Place bowl over another bowl filled with ice cubes and water to chill until mixture is slightly thickened.

9. To assemble, pour half the strawberry mousse into lined cake ring and place strawberry disc on top. Press lightly. Top with remaining mousse and smoothen it out using a straight spatula. Refrigerate to set.

10. Warm sides of cake ring with a warm towel or blowtorch to unmold cake.

11. Make whipped cream. Combine whipping cream, sugar and chery liqueur in a clean bowl. Place bowl over another bowl filled with ice cubes and water. Using an electric mixer, whisk cream at medium speed until soft peaks form. Spoon whipped cream into a piping bag fitted with a star piping tip.

12. Pipe cream on cake and garnish with berries. Slice and serve.

red berry roll cake

Makes one 28-cm roll cake

 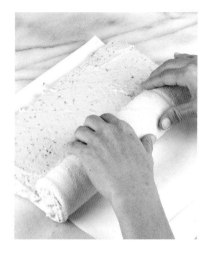 

Coconut meringue 50 g (page 106)

Red berries

SOUFFLÉ ROLL SPONGE

Egg 1

Egg yolks 3

Vanilla extract 1 tsp

Unsalted butter 35 g

Pastry flour 60 g, sifted twice

Fresh whole milk 60 g

Egg whites 3

Castor sugar 90 g

STRAWBERRY CREAM

Strawberries 80 g

Whipping cream (35% fat) 120 g

Raspberry purée 15 g

Castor sugar 20 g

WHIPPED CREAM

Whipping cream (35% fat) 120 g

Castor sugar 2 tsp

Kirsch (cherry liqueur) ¹/₂ Tbsp

1. Make coconut meringue in advance. Pipe meringue in lines using a 1-cm round tip.

2. Preheat oven to 180°C. Line a 28-cm square Swiss roll cake pan with parchment paper.

3. Make soufflé roll sponge. Combine egg, egg yolks and vanilla in a small bowl and beat lightly. Set aside. Place butter in a small saucepan and heat gently until melted. Add flour to melted butter and cook through. Transfer mixture to a bowl and add beaten eggs a little at a time, mixing with a spatula until batter is smooth. Add milk and mix to incorporate. Strain batter and set aside.

4. Make meringue. Beat egg whites in a clean bowl until foamy. Add half the sugar and continue beating for a few minutes, then add remaining sugar and beat until stiff peaks form and meringue is glossy.

5. Add one-third of meringue to egg batter and fold in lightly. Add remaining meringue and fold through until just incorporated.

6. Pour batter into prepared cake pan and spread evenly with a scraper. Place cake pan on a tray and bake for 20 minutes. When sponge is done, remove from heat and place in a big plastic bag to cool. When sponge is cooled, peel away layer of brown skin on surface. Trim one edge of cake diagonally.

7. Make strawberry cream. Cut strawberries into small pieces. Place whipping cream, strawberries, raspberry pure and sugar in a bowl. Place bowl over another bowl filled with ice cubes and water. Using an electric mixer, whisk cream at medium speed until stiff peaks form and cream is smooth.

SUGAR SYRUP

Water 30 g

Castor sugar 15 g

Kirsch (cherry liqueur) 1 Tbsp

NOTE: You can also just use plain whipped cream for this Swiss roll, and/or make a chocolate soufflé sponge. To make a chocolate soufflé sponge, reduce flour to 50 g and add 10 g cocoa powder. Increase sugar to 100 g.

8. Make whipped cream. Combine whipped cream, sugar and kirsch in a bowl and beat as for strawberry cream.

9. Make sugar syrup. Combine water, sugar and kirsch in a bowl and mix well.

10. To assemble, place sponge on a sheet of parchment paper. The slanted side of the sponge should be away from you. Brush sponge with syrup, then spread evenly with strawberry cream. Gently roll up sponge to make a Swiss roll. Place in the freezer until roll is set. Cover with whipped cream, and decorate with coconut meringue and red berries. Slice and serve immediately.

raspberry chiffon cake

Makes one 20-cm round cake

Frozen raspberries 80 g

Pastry flour 1 Tbsp + 90 g

Egg yolks 5

Castor sugar 20 g

Fresh whole milk 60 g

Vegetable oil 60 g

MERINGUE

Castor sugar 90 g

Cornflour 10 g

Egg whites 180 g, about 5 eggs

WHIPPED CREAM

Whipping cream (35% fat) 200 g

Castor sugar 1 Tbsp

RASPBERRY CREAM

Whipping cream (35% fat) 200 g

Castor sugar 25 g

Raspberry purée 40 g

NOTE: When the baked chiffon cake is cut, you may notice large holes near the pieces of raspberry. Since fresh raspberries hold lots of moisture, this is quite normal.

1. Preheat oven to 160°C. Prepare an ungreased 20-cm chiffon cake tube pan. Break up frozen raspberries into small pieces with your fingers, then coat with 1 Tbsp flour. Place in the freezer until needed.

2. Sift 90 g flour twice. Combine egg yolks and sugar in a bowl and mix well. Add milk and oil and mix again. Add flour and mix until batter becomes sticky. Set aside.

3. Make meringue. Combine sugar and cornflour. Beat egg whites until foamy. Add half the sugar mixture and continue beating for a few minutes, then add remaining sugar mixture and beat until stiff peaks form and meringue is glossy.

4. Add one-third of meringue to egg yolk mixture and fold in lightly, then add remaining meringue and fold to incorporate completely. Add frozen raspberries and fold gently.

5. Pour batter into chiffon cake tube pan. Bake for 40–50 minutes. When cake is done, remove from oven and turn it over to cool.

6. Make whipped cream. Place whipping cream and sugar in a clean bowl, then place bowl over another bowl filled with ice cubes and water. Using an electric mixer, whisk cream at medium speed until stiff peaks form and cream is smooth.

7. Cover cake with whipped cream using a spatula and decorating turntable.

8. Make raspberry cream. Combine ingredients in a clean bowl and whisk as with whipped cream. Spoon into a piping bag fitted with an open star tip and pipe roses on cake. Decorate with raspberries. Slice and serve.

yoghurt cream biscuit roll cake

Makes one 27-cm roll cake

A selection of fresh fruit
(kiwi, strawberries, raspberries, mangoes and bananas or canned fruit such as pears and yellow peaches)

BISCUIT SPONGE

Eggs 3

Castor sugar 90 g

Vanilla extract 1 tsp

Pastry flour 90 g, sifted twice

Icing sugar as needed

YOGHURT CREAM

Yoghurt 200 g

Whipping cream (35% fat) 200 g

Castor sugar 20 g

WHIPPED CREAM

Whipping cream (35% fat) 100 g

Castor sugar 2 tsp

NOTE: You can use any flavour of whipped cream and vary the selection of fruit in the roll cake.

1. Leave yoghurt (for making yoghurt cream) to drain in a coffee filter and dripper in the refrigerator for at least 3 hours until yoghurt is about 100 g.

2. Preheat oven to 200°C. Line a 28-cm square Swiss roll cake pan with parchment paper.

3. Make biscuit sponge. Separate egg whites and yolks. Beat yolks lightly and add half the sugar and vanilla. Whisk until mixture thickens and becomes pale.

4. Make meringue. Place egg whites in a clean bowl and beat until foamy. Add remaining sugar and beat until stiff peaks form and meringue is glossy.

5. Add one-third of meringue into egg yolk mixture and fold lightly. Add flour and fold well, then add remaining meringue and fold through until just incorporated.

6. Spoon batter into a piping bag fitted with a 1-cm round piping tip. Pipe diagonal lines to fill cake pan. (Any extra batter can be used to make finger-shaped biscuit sponges.) Dust batter twice with icing sugar, then bake for 7–10 minutes. Remove cake from pan and place on a wire rack to cool.

7. Make yoghurt cream. Combine whipping cream and sugar into a clean bowl. Place over another bowl filled with ice cubes and water. Using an electric mixer, whisk cream at medium speed until stiff peaks form and cream is smooth. Add drained yoghurt and mix well.

8. Assemble biscuit roll. Turn cooled cake onto a clean work surface. Peel off parchment paper and spread with an even layer of yoghurt cream. Arrange your choice of fruit on cream, then gently roll up. Cover with cling wrap and chill in the freezer for about 10 minutes.

9. Make whipped cream. Combine ingredients in a clean bowl and whisk as with yoghurt cream. Spoon cream into a piping bag fitted with a 1-cm star tip. Pipe cream to decorate cake, then top with your choice of fruit.

rum chocolate cake pops

Makes about 20 cake pops

GENOISE SPONGE

Eggs 170 g

Castor sugar 130 g

Glucose 15 g

Pastry flour 115 g, sifted twice

Unsalted butter 30 g

Fresh whole milk 45 g

Vanilla extract 1/2 tsp

RUM BALLS

Genoise sponge crumbs 300 g

Whipping cream (35% fat) 40 g

Dark sweet chocolate (55% cocoa)
  40 g, chopped into small pieces

Rum 2 tsp

RUM RAISINS

Raisins 90 g

Rum 50 g

COATING AND DECORATION

Coating chocolate 400 g,
  chopped into small pieces

Sugar decorations

1. Make rum raisins a day in advance. Boil raisins in a small pot of water and strain. Pat dry using paper towels, then soak overnight in rum. Drain and pat dry, then cut into small pieces. Set aside.

2. Preheat oven to 160°C. Line an 18-cm round cake pan with parchment paper. Using a clean bowl, beat eggs with an electric whisk, then add sugar and glucose. Place bowl over a double boiler and beat well. When egg mixture is warm, beat at high speed until light and fluffy. Reduce speed to low and continue beating for about 1 minute. Gently fold in flour with a spatula.

3. Combine butter, milk and vanilla in a bowl and place over a double boiler. Once butter has melted, stir through to mix. Add one-fifth of egg batter to butter mixture and mix well. Add butter mixture to remaining egg batter and fold through evenly.

4. Pour batter into prepared cake pan and bake for 45–50 minutes or until cake springs back when touched. Remove from pan and place on a wire rack in a big plastic bag to cool. When cool, place sponge into a food processor and pulse to get crumbs. Measure out 300 g crumbs to make rum balls. (Remaining crumbs will keep for up to 1 month in the freezer.)

5. Make chocolate ganache for rum balls. Place cream in a saucepan and bring to a boil over medium heat. Once cream boils, remove from heat. Place chocolate in a bowl and pour hot cream over. Let mixture sit for 30 seconds, then stir with a spatula until smooth. Set aside to cool.

NOTE: Cake pops make a lovely gift for any occasion. As a variation to this recipe, you can add nuts to the mixture and dip the balls in melted white chocolate.

6. Make rum balls. Place crumbs, rum raisins, chocolate ganache and rum into a bowl and mix well. Place 25 g mixture in a small sheet of cling film and form into a ball. Place on a tray. Repeat until ingredients are used up. Place rum balls in the freezer for about 15 minutes.

7. Melt coating chocolate in a heatproof bowl over a double boiler.

8. Dip one end of a cake pop stick into melted chocolate and push into an unwrapped rum ball. Dip rum ball into chocolate to coat, then sprinkle with sugar decorations. Stick cake pop into a polystyrene foam block to set. Repeat with remaining cake pops.

flower cupcakes

Makes 6 cupcakes

Pastry flour 90 g

Baking powder ¹/₂ tsp

Egg 1

Castor sugar 65 g

Whipping cream (35% fat) 100 g

Vanilla extract ¹/₂ tsp

Strawberry jam about 2 Tbsp

BUTTERCREAM

Unsalted butter 200 g,
    at room temperature

Egg whites 70 g

Icing sugar 70 g

Orange liqueur 1 Tbsp

**Pink, blue, green and yellow
    icing colours**

NOTE: Be creative when decorating the cupcakes. Further details about piping flowers using buttercream can be found in my first book, *Okashi*, page 118.

1. Preheat oven 170°C. Line a 6-hole muffin tray with paper cupcake cases.

2. Sift flour and baking powder together twice. Set aside. Place egg in a bowl and beat lightly. Add sugar and beat well until a little fluffy. Add whipping cream and vanilla. Mix well. Gently fold in flour with a spatula until just incorporated. Spoon batter into a piping bag fitted with 1-cm round piping tip. Pipe batter into cupcake cases until half full, then top each one with 1 tsp strawberry jam and continue to fill cases with batter until 90% full.

3. Bake for about 30 minutes, then remove from tray and place on a wire rack to cool.

4. Make buttercream. Beat butter until pale and creamy using an electric mixer. In a clean bowl, beat egg whites until foamy. Add half the icing sugar and continue beating. When egg whites have achieved some volume, add remaining icing sugar and continue to beat until stiff peaks form and meringue is glossy. Add to creamed butter and mix thoroughly. Add orange liqueur and fold in well.

5. Divide buttercream into 3 equal portions, then subdivide 2 portions in half. Leave largest portion plain. Colour each of the other 4 portions pink, blue, green and yellow using icing colours. Spoon buttercreams into separate piping bags fitted with piping tips and pipe flowers and spirals on cupcakes. For flowers, I used petal piping tips and plain, pink, blue and yellow buttercreams. For leaves, I used a leaf piping tip and green buttercream. For spirals, I used round piping tips. Just have fun and decorate the cupcakes in any way you like.

chocolate raspberry mousse cake

Makes a 24-cm rectangular cake

CHOCOLATE ROLL SPONGE

Pastry flour 35 g

Cocoa powder 15 g

Eggs 3

Castor sugar 80 g

BAVARIAN CREAM

Fresh whole milk 120 g

Vanilla bean 1/2, pod split and
seeds scraped

Egg yolks 2

Castor sugar 45 g

Gelatin sheets 8 g, soaked in
iced water to soften

Whipping cream (35% fat) 120 g

Kirsch (cherry liqueur) 1/2 Tbsp

RASPBERRY JELLY

Raspberry purée 100 g

Castor sugar 30 g

Gelatin sheets 8 g, soaked in
iced water to soften

1. Make raspberry jelly a day in advance. Place raspberry purée and sugar in a bowl and mix well until sugar is dissolved. Place softened gelatin in a small bowl and melt over a double boiler. Add to raspberry mixture and mix well. Line a 11-cm square container with cling wrap and pour raspberry mixture into it. Place in the freezer overnight. Remove jelly from container and cut into small cubes. Store in the freezer until needed.

2. Preheat oven to 200°C. Line a 28-cm square Swiss roll cake pan with parchment paper and a 24 x 5.5-cm half spherical rectangular pan with cling film.

3. Make chocolate roll sponge. Sift flour and cocoa powder together twice. Set aside. Using a clean bowl, beat eggs with a whisk. Add sugar, then place bowl over a double boiler and mix well. When egg mixture is warm, use an electric mixer and beat at high speed until light and fluffy. Reduce speed to low and continue beating for about 1 minute. Gently fold in flour mixture with a spatula. Pour batter into prepared cake pan and spread evenly with a scraper. Place cake pan on a tray and bake for 10–13 minutes. When sponge is done, remove from pan and place in a big plastic bag to cool.

4. Make sugar syrup. Combine water, sugar and chery liqueur in a bowl and mix well.

5. Remove skin from top of sponge, then cut to get 2 rectangular sheets: 24 ×15.5-cm and 24 × 6.5-cm. Place larger sheet into half spherical pan and brush with about two-thirds of syrup. Set aside.

6. Make Bavarian cream. Heat milk with vanilla pod and seeds, and half the sugar in a saucepan over low heat. In a clean bowl, beat egg yolks and

CHOCOLATE GLAZE

Water 50 g

Castor sugar 85 g

Cocoa powder 35 g

Whipping cream (35% fat) 50 g

Gelatin sheets 5 g, soaked in
   iced water to soften

SUGAR SYRUP

Water 20 g

Castor sugar 10 g

Kirsch (cherry liqueur) ¹/₂ tsp

NOTE: This recipe can also be used to
make a simple chocolate roll cake with
Bavarian cream and fresh fruit.

remaining sugar until light. Add little of the warm milk and mix well. Add egg mixture to remaining milk in saucepan and cook over gentle heat, stirring continuously until mixture thickens. Remove vanilla pod from mixture. Add softened gelatin to saucepan and stir to dissolve. Transfer custard to a mixing bowl and place over a larger bowl half-filled with iced water to cool slightly. (Be careful not to chill mixture too much.)

7. Pour whipping cream into a clean bowl. Place bowl over another bowl filled with ice cubes and water. Using an electric mixer, whisk cream at medium speed until stiff peaks form and cream is smooth. Add whipped cream to custard mixture and fold through.

8. Pour half the Bavarian cream into half spherical pan and add raspberry jelly cubes. Pour remaining Bavarian cream to cover jelly.

9. Brush remaining syrup on one side of smaller chocolate sponge sheet and place it syrup-side down on cream. Place in the freezer for about 30 minutes to an hour to set.

10. When cake is set, remove from pan and place on a wire rack on a tray to glaze.

11. Make chocolate graze. Combine water, sugar, cocoa powder and whipping cream in a saucepan and mix well. Cook over gentle heat, stirring continuously until mixture boils. Add softened gelatin and mix well until gelatin is dissolved. Strain mixture into a clean bowl and place over another bowl filled with ice cubes and water until glaze thickens a little. If glaze becomes too thick, melt it by putting the bowl in hot water. Pour chocolate glaze over chilled cake. Decorate with berries. Slice to serve.

bavarian cream cake with fruit

Makes one 18-cm round cake

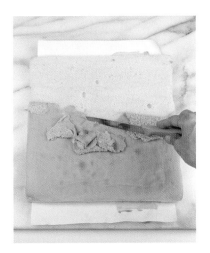  

A selection of fruit (such as canned pears, canned yellow peaches, fresh raspberries and fresh blueberries)

BISCUIT SPONGE

Pastry flour 40 g

Cornflour 20 g

Egg whites 90 g

Castor sugar 80 g

Egg yolks 80 g

Unsalted butter 35 g, melted

Vanilla extract 1 tsp

BAVARIAN CREAM

Fresh whole milk 125 g

Vanilla bean 1/2, pod split and seeds scraped

Castor sugar 35 g

Egg yolks 2

Gelatin sheets 6 g, soaked in iced water to soften

Whipping cream (35% fat) 100 g

1. Make cake a day in advance. Cover one side of an 18-cm cake ring with cling film and place on a tray. Fit an 18-cm round cakeboard into cake ring. Line a 28-cm square Swiss roll pan with parchment paper.

2. Preheat oven to 200°C. Make biscuit sponge. Sift flour and cornflour together twice. Set aside. Place egg whites in a clean bowl and beat until foamy. Add a quarter of sugar and beat for a while, then add remaining sugar and beat until stiff peaks form and meringue is glossy. Add egg yolks to meringue and mix well. Fold in sifted flour mixture using a spatula. Add melted butter and vanilla and fold well.

3. Pour batter into Swiss roll pan and spread evenly with a scraper. Place pan on a tray and bake for 10–13 minutes. Remove cake from pan and place in a big plastic bag to cool.

4. Peel brown skin from top of cooled biscuit sponge and cut out an 18-cm round piece. Place this into the 18-cm cake ring.

5. Make Kirsch sugar syrup. Combine ingredients and mix well. Brush syrup over biscuit sponge. Set aside.

6. Make Bavarian cream. Heat milk with vanilla pod and seeds, and half the sugar in a saucepan over low heat. In a clean bowl, beat egg yolks and remaining sugar until a light emulsion is formed. Add a little of the warm milk to egg mixture and mix well, then pour mixture into saucepan and continue cooking over gentle heat, stirring until mixture thickens. Add gelatin and stir well. Strain mixture into a bowl, then place bowl over another bowl filled with ice cubes and water to cool cream to body temperature (not cold).

JELLY

Water 250 g

Castor sugar 40 g

Gelatin sheets 8 g , soaked in
iced water to soften

Kirsch (cherry liqueur) 1 Tbsp

KIRSCH SUGAR SYRUP

Water 15 g

Castor sugar 8 g

Kirsch (cherry liqueur) ¹/₂ tsp

NOTE: The Bavarian cream can be set in
glasses and served as a dessert on its own.
This recipe makes enough for 5 servings.

7. Place whipping cream in a clean bowl over another bowl filled with ice cubes
    and water. Using an electric mixer, whisk cream on medium speed until
    stiff peaks form and cream is smooth. Fold whipped cream into cooled cream,
    mixing thoroughly.

8. Pour Bavarian cream over biscuit sponge, and place in the freezer for 20–
    30 minutes until set.

9. Make jelly. Place water and sugar in a small saucepan and bring to a boil.
    Add gelatin and mix well. Strain syrup into a bowl, and place bowl over another
    bowl filled with ice cubes and water to cool jelly, but not set it. Add Kirsch and
    mix well.

10. Arrange fruit on set Bavarian cream, then pour jelly over. Refrigerate overnight.

11. To unmould cake, heat sides of cake ring with a warm towel or a blowtorch.
    Cut into even pieces and serve.

coconut milk cake

Makes one 16-cm round cake

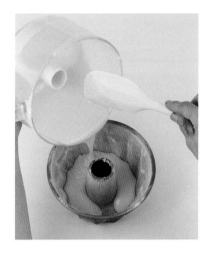  

Pastry flour 50 g

Baking powder 1/2 tsp

Castor sugar 100 g

Coconut milk powder 60 g

Eggs 2 (about 100 g)

Rum 2 tsp

Unsalted butter 40 g, melted

Finely grated coconut 70 g

White chocolate 70 g, chopped

NOTE: This cake has a lovely milky coconut flavour due to the coconut milk powder. To vary this recipe, try coating the cake with dark chocolate instead of white chocolate.

1. Grease a 16-cm Gugelhupf mould with a little softened butter, then place in the freezer to chill. Dust mould with some flour, then tap to remove excess flour. Set aside.

2. Preheat oven to 170°C. Sift flour and baking powder together twice.

3. Place sugar and coconut milk powder into a bowl and mix well. Add eggs and rum and mix thoroughly. Fold in sifted flour, then add melted butter and mix well.

4. Pour batter into prepared Gugelhupf mould and bake for 40–45 minutes. Remove cake from mould and leave on a wire rack to cool.

5. Spread grated coconut out on a baking tray and bake for 15 minutes at 150°C without preheating oven.

6. Place chopped white chocolate in a bowl and heat over a double boiler until chocolate is melted. Brush white chocolate all over cake, then coat with baked grated coconut. Slice and serve.

orange flower cake

Makes one 16-cm round cake

Unsalted butter 90 g,
  at room temperature

Icing sugar 45 g

Salt a pinch

Egg yolks 3

Fresh whole milk 2 Tbsp

Pastry flour 90 g, sifted

Ground almonds 40 g

Sliced candied orange 90 g

MERINGUE

Egg whites 2 (about 70 g)

Icing sugar 45 g

SUGAR GLAZE

Icing sugar 70 g

Lemon juice 2 tsp

Orange liqueur 1 tsp

ICING FLOWERS

Icing sugar 250 g

Egg whites 40 g

Orange and yellow icing colours

1. Make icing flowers a day in advance. Beat icing sugar and egg whites in a bowl until texture is firm. Divide icing into 3 equal portions. Using just a little colouring, colour one portion orange and another yellow. Leave one plain.

2. Spoon icing into separate piping bags fitted with petal piping tips. To pipe 5-petal flowers, start by applying a little icing on a flower nail and place a piece of waxed paper on it. Hold piping bag at a 45° angle, with the wide end of the tip touching the paper. Pipe a petal while rotating the piping bag clockwise and rotating the nail counterclockwise. Do this 4 times to make 5 petals, each petal overlapping slightly. Pipe flower centre using a small round tip. Pipe enough flowers to decorate cake. Leave on a tray to dry completely overnight.

3. Grease a 16-cm Gugelhupf mould with a little softened butter, then place in the freezer to chill. Dust mould with some flour, then tap to remove excess flour. Set aside.

4. Preheat oven to 170°C. Place butter, icing sugar and salt in a bowl and beat until creamy. Add egg yolks and milk and beat until light and fluffy.

5. Make meringue. In a clean bowl, beat egg whites until foamy, then add icing sugar and beat until stiff peaks form and meringue is glossy.

6. Add one-third of meringue to butter mixture and fold in lightly. Add sifted flour, ground almonds and candid orange, and fold through with a spatula. Add remaining meringue and fold to incorporate completely. The batter should be glossy and smooth.

NOTE: This decorated cake makes a lovely present for any occasion. The colour of the icing flowers can be changed to suit your theme.

7. Pour batter into prepared mould and bake for 40–45 minutes. Remove cake from pan and leave to cool on a wire rack.

8. Make sugar grale. Place icing sugar, lemon juice and orange liqueur in a small bowl and mix well. Pour glaze over cake and decorate with icing flowers.

coffee rum praline ring cake

Makes one 18-cm ring cake

Unsalted butter 120 g,
   at room temperature

Icing sugar 100 g

Eggs 120 g

Pastry flour 120 g

Baking powder a pinch

BUTTERCREAM

Instant coffee powder 5 g

Rum ½ Tbsp

Unsalted butter 150 g,
   at room temperature

Egg whites 55 g

Icing sugar 55 g

RUM RAISINS

Raisins 20 g

Rum 10 g

PRALINE

Blanched almond slivers 50 g

Castor sugar 70 g

1. Make rum raisins a day in advance. Boil raisins in a small pot of water and strain. Pat dry using paper towels, then soak overnight in rum. Drain and pat dry. Reserve a few whole raisins for decorating cake, then cut the rest into small pieces. Set aside.

2. Bake almond slivers for praline. Place on a baking tray and bake for 20 minutes at 160°C without preheating oven. Set aside.

3. Preheat oven to 170°C. Lightly grease an 18-cm ring pan with a little softened butter, then place in the freezer to chill. Dust pan with some flour, then tap to remove excess flour. Set aside. Sift flour and baking powder together twice.

4. Make syrup. Place water, sugar and rum in a small bowl and mix well.

5. Beat butter and icing sugar with an electric mixer until light, fluffy and pale. Gradually add eggs and beat well. Add flour mixture and fold through completely using a spatula. The batter should be glossy and smooth. Pour batter into prepared ring pan and bake for about 40 minutes. Remove cake from pan and place on a wire rack to cool.

6. Make praline. Heat sugar in a saucepan until caramelised. Add almond slivers and mix quickly. Pour out on a lined tray and let cool. Chop praline into tiny pieces. Set aside.

7. Make buttercream. Mix coffee powder with rum and set aside. Using an electric mixer, beat butter for about 10 minutes until pale and creamy. In a clean bowl, beat egg whites until foamy. Add half the icing sugar and beat until egg whites have achieved some volume. Add remaining sugar and beat

SYRUP

Water 20 g

Castor sugar 10 g

Rum ¼ tsp

NOTE: This cake is a combination several basic recipes. You may use these basic recipes separately and change the flavour to suit your taste. Butter cakes are best served at room temperature. If storing in the refrigerator, bring it to room temperature by heating in the microwave oven at 600 w for 15 seconds before serving.

until stiff peaks form and meringue is glossy. Add meringue to whipped butter and mix thoroughly. Add coffee-rum mixture and fold in well.

8. Slice cake horizontally to get 3 layers. Place 1 layer on a flat tray and brush evenly with syrup. Spread with some buttercream, top with half the rum raisins and spread with more buttercream. Brush a second layer of cake with syrup and arrange on layer of buttercream. Repeat to layer cake, then top with the final layer of cake. Brush remaining syrup over cake, then cover with buttercream.

9. Spoon remaining buttercream into a piping bag fitted with a star piping tip.

10. Coat cake with chopped praline, then pipe cream to decorate. Top with reserved rum raisins. Slice and serve at room temperature.

cream soufflé with chocolate ganache

Makes 4 servings

Unsalted butter 20 g

Pastry flour 30 g, sifted

Whole fresh milk 200 g

Salt a pinch

Egg yolks 3

MERINGUE

Castor sugar 45 g

Cornflour 10 g

Egg whites 140 g (about 4 eggs)

CHOCOLATE GANACHE

Whipping cream (35% fat) 100 g

Dark couverture chocolate 70 g,
chopped into small pieces

NOTE: This cream soufflé can also be
enjoyed on its own without chocolate
ganache. As a variation to this recipes,
you can flavour the soufflé with half a vanilla
pod/1 tsp vanilla extract or with fruit sauce.

1. Preheat oven 170°C. Lightly grease four 9-cm diameter ramekins with softened butter and dust with castor sugar.

2. Place butter in a small saucepan and melt over medium heat. Reduce to low heat and add flour, stirring well with a spatula.

3. Pour milk and salt into another small saucepan and bring to a boil. Add hot milk gradually to flour mixture and cook over gentle heat, stirring continuously until mixture leaves sides of saucepan and becomes very thick. Transfer to a bowl and add egg yolks. Mix well.

4. Make meringue. Combine sugar and cornflour in a small bowl and mix well. In a clean bowl, beat egg whites until foamy. Add sugar mixture and beat until stiff peaks form and meringue is glossy.

5. Add one-third of meringue to egg yolk mixture and fold in lightly. Add remaining meringue and fold in completely. Pour batter into ramekins and level with a spatula. Run the tip of your thumb around the edge of each ramekin to create a groove between the batter and edge of ramekin.

6. Place ramekins in a deep baking tray and add enough hot water to come 1 cm up the sides of ramekins. Bake for 20–25 minutes or until soufflés are risen and golden.

7. Make chocolate ganache. Boil whipping cream in a saucepan over medium heat, then pour over chocolate. Let mixture sit for 30 seconds, then stir with a spatula until smooth.

8. Dust soufflés with icing sugar. Serve immediately with warm chocolate ganache.

mango coconut cheesecake

Makes 10 small cakes

Pastry flour 40 g

Cornflour 20 g

Vanilla extract 1 tsp

Unsalted butter 35 g

Egg whites 90 g

Castor sugar 80 g

Egg yolks 5 (about 80 g)

MANGO COCONUT CREAM

Cream cheese 150 g

Castor sugar 40 g

Coconut cream 60 g

Whipping cream (35% fat) 100 g

Mango purée 200 g

Gelatin sheets 9 g, soaked in
  iced water to soften

NOTE: This recipe can also be made into
an 18-cm round cake. Cut sponge into an
18-cm disc and place into an 18-cm cake
ring wrapped with cling wrap. Pour cream
cheese into cake ring to set.

1. Preheat oven to 200°C. Line a 28-cm square Swiss roll pan with parchment paper. Prepare a silicon mould with 7-cm cavities.

2. Sift flour and cornflour together twice. Set aside. Add vanilla extract into butter, then melt over a double boiler or in a microwave oven. Set aside.

3. Place egg whites in a clean bowl and beat until foamy. Add a quarter of sugar and beat for a while, then add remaining sugar and beat until stiff peaks form and meringue is glossy. Add egg yolks and mix well. Add flour mixture and fold in using a spatula. Add melted butter and fold well.

4. Pour batter into prepared pan and spread evenly with a scraper. Place pan on a tray and bake for 10–13 minutes. Remove cake from pan and place in a big bag to cool.

5. Peel brown skin from sponge and use a 4.5-cm round cutter to cut 10 discs from sponge. Set aside.

6. Make mango coconut cream. Microwave cream cheese for 30 seconds at 600 w to soften. Add sugar and mix well. Add coconut cream, whipping cream and mango purée and mix again until well incorporated.

7. Place softened gelatin in a small bowl and melt over a double boiler. Add to cream cheese mixture and mix well.

8. Spoon cream cheese mixture into each cavity in silicon mould until it is about 90% full. Press a sponge disc lightly into each mould.

9. Place in the freezer to set overnight. Remove from mould and defrost for a few hours in the refrigerator before serving.

baked oreo cheesecake

Makes one 18-cm round cake

BASE

Oreo cookies, cream removed 100 g

Unsalted butter 40 g, melted

CREAM CHEESE LAYER

Cream cheese 370 g

Sour cream 150 g

Castor sugar 120 g

Cornflour 10 g

Unsalted butter 30 g,
   at room temperature

Egg 1

Egg yolks 2

Vanilla extract 1 tsp

Lemon 1, rind finely grated

RED BERRY SAUCE

Strawberries 170 g

Raspberries 150 g

Castor sugar 65 g

Lemon juice 2 tsp

NOTE: To vary this recipe, use wheat crackers instead of Oreos. This cheesecake can also be served on its own without the red berry sauce.

1. Make cheesecake a day in advance. Prepare an 18-cm round cake pan with a removal base and grease lightly with softened butter.

2. Make base. Lightly pulse cookies into fine crumbs. Add melted butter and mix well. Transfer crumbs to cake pan and spread evenly. Press down to pack crumbs tightly together using the base of a glass cup. Place in the freezer to set.

3. Preheat oven 160°C.

4. Microwave cream cheese at 600 w for 30 seconds or until softened. Place in a food processor with sour cream, sugar, cornflour and butter and blend well. Add egg and egg yolks and blend again. Add vanilla and lemon rind and blend well.

5. Pour cream cheese mixture into prepared pan. Place pan in a slightly larger pan or wrap bottom tightly with aluminium foil, and place into a deep baking tray. Add enough hot water to come 1–2 cm up the side of pan. Bake for 70–80 minutes until surface of cheesecake is dark brown.

6. Leave cheesecake to cool on a wire rack, then cover with a paper towel and cling film, and chill in the refrigerator overnight.

7. Make red berry sauce. Place strawberries, raspberries, sugar and lemon juice in a saucepan and cook over medium heat for 3–5 minutes until slightly thickened. Using a stick blender, blend lightly to get a thick sauce.

8. To unmould cake, warm side of cake pan with a warm towel or a blowtorch. Slice and serve with red berry sauce.

mini lemon cream puffs

Makes about 20 mini cream puffs

CHOUX PASTRY

Water 70 g

Unsalted butter 25 g

Castor sugar a pinch

Salt a pinch

Pastry flour 40 g, sifted

Eggs 1–2, lightly beaten

LEMON CREAM

Fresh whole milk 200 g

Egg yolks 3

Castor sugar 70 g

Pastry flour 20 g

Unsalted butter 20 g

Lemon juice 20 g

Lemon 1, rind grated finely

Whipping cream (45% fat) 1 Tbsp

SUGAR GLAZE

Icing sugar 120 g

Lemon juice about 20 g

Yellow icing colour 1–2 drops

TOPPING

Pistachio nuts, chopped

1. Preheat oven to 200°C. Line a baking tray with parchment paper.

2. Make choux pastry. In a small pan, combine water, butter, sugar and salt. Bring to a boil over medium-high heat, then immediately remove from heat.

3. Using a wooden spoon, quickly stir in flour until combined and mixture comes together in a ball. Return to heat and cook, stirring constantly until mixture leaves sides of the pan and a film forms on the bottom of pan.

4. Transfer mixture to a clean bowl. Add one egg a little at a time, beating with a wooden spoon until egg is fully incorporated. (Alternatively, use an electric mixer fitted with a paddle attachment.)

5. Test if batter is ready by scooping it up using a wooden spoon. The batter should hang down and form a smooth triangular shape. If it does not, the batter needs a little more egg.

6. Pour batter into a piping bag fitted with a 1-cm round piping tip. Pipe 2.5-cm circles onto prepared tray and gently smoothen out pointed peaks with a moistened finger.

7. Bake for 12–15 minutes, then reduce temperature to 180°C and bake for another 20 minutes. Remove from heat and place on a wire rack to cool.

8. Make lemon cream. Bring milk to a boil in a pan. In a clean bowl, beat egg yolks and sugar together until mixture is pale. Add flour and mix well. Add hot milk to egg mixture and fold through. Return egg and milk mixture to pan and bring to a boil over high heat, stirring constantly until mixture is smooth and glossy. Remove pan from heat. Add butter, lemon juice and lemon rind and mix well. Pour cream on a tray, cover with cling wrap and

NOTE: This choux pastry recipe can also be used to make *chouquettes*, a simple, but very yummy French snack. After piping the dough, sprinkle with pearl sugar and bake. *Chouquettes* are made without any filling.

place in the freezer to cool, but not freeze it. Before use, gently beat cream with an electric mixer until smooth and creamy, then add whipping cream and mix thoroughly. Spoon lemon cream into a piping bag fitted with a 5-mm round piping tip.

9. Push a 2-mm piping tip into the base of a choux puff and pipe enough lemon cream to fill it. Repeat to fill all choux puffs.

10. Make sugar glaze. Place icing sugar and lemon juice in a small bowl and mix well. Add a little yellow icing colour.

11. Dip top of each choux puff in sugar glaze and sprinkle with chopped pistachios. Serve.

caramel fudge brownie

Makes one 20-cm square cake

Walnuts 50 g

Pecans 50 g

Dark sweet chocolate (55% cocoa)
  150 g, chopped

Cocoa mass 50 g, chopped

Unsalted butter 90 g

Castor sugar 120 g

Eggs 120 g (about 2 eggs)

Egg yolk 1

Vanilla extract 1 tsp

Salt a pinch

Pastry flour 50 g, sifted

CARAMEL CREAM

Castor sugar 50 g

Glucose 40 g

Salt a pinch

Whipping cream (35% fat) 50 g

NOTE: This brownie can be enjoyed on its own without the caramel cream. The caramel cream can also be used as a topping for ice cream, scones, cookies and bread.

1. Spread walnuts and pecans out on a flat baking tray and bake for 20 minutes at 160°C without preheating oven. Chop nuts into small pieces. Reserve some for topping.

2. Preheat oven to 170°C. Line a 20-cm square cake pan with parchment paper.

3. Place chocolate, cocoa mass and butter in a heatproof bowl and melt over a double boiler. Add sugar, eggs, egg yolk, vanilla extract and salt and mix well using a whisk. Add flour and chopped nuts and fold thoroughly.

4. Pour batter into prepared cake pan and top with reserved nuts. Bake for 25–30 minutes. Remove cake from pan and leave on a wire rack to cool.

5. Make caramel cream. Place sugar, glucose and salt in a saucepan and heat until sugar caramelises. Turn off heat and carefully pour whipping cream into saucepan while stirring with a spatula, mixing until smooth. Leave to cool slightly.

6. Drizzle caramel cream over brownie and leave to cool. Slice and serve.

lemon tart

Makes one 20-cm round tart

Chopped pistachios

SWEET SHORTCRUST PASTRY

Unsalted butter 70 g,
 at room temperature

Icing sugar 35 g

Salt a pinch

Vanilla extract 1/2 tsp

Eggs 20 g

Ground almonds 20 g

Pastry flour 130 g

LEMON CREAM

Unsalted butter 100 g

Castor sugar 170 g

Lemons 2, rind finely grated;
 squeezed for 90 g juice

Egg 2

Egg yolks 3

Gelatin sheets 2.5 g, soaked in
 iced water to soften

1. Make sweet shortcrust pastry. Beat butter, icing sugar, salt and vanilla
    with an electric mixer until just combined. Add eggs and beat well.
    Add ground almonds and mix well. Add flour and fold through completely.
    Using a bench scraper, mix batter until a smooth dough is formed.

2. Place dough on a non-stick baking mat. Cover surface with cling wrap
    and roll out into a 3–5-mm thick sheet. Transfer to a tray and refrigerate
    for about 30 minutes. Remove non-stick baking mat and place dough
    (with cling wrap still intact) into a 20-cm fluted tart tin with a removable
    base. Press dough gently into tin without stretching it. Remove and
    discard cling wrap.

3. Roll a rolling pin over the top of the tin to remove excess dough. Prick
    dough with a fork and let rest for 5 minutes in the freezer.

4. Preheat oven to 180°C. Place some parchment paper or a non-stick
    baking mat over dough. Place baking weights into tart tin and bake for
    20 minutes. Remove weights and parchment paper or baking mat when
    pastry just begins to colour around the edges and continue baking for
    another 10 minutes until light golden brown. Remove from heat and leave
    to cool on a wire rack.

5. Make lemon cream. Heat butter, 100 g sugar and lemon juice in a
    saucepan over low heat. Place eggs, egg yolks and remaining sugar in
    a bowl and mix well. Add butter mixture to egg mixture and mix well.
    Add to saucepan and cook over gentle heat, stirring until mixture thickens.
    Add softened gelatin and mix through.

WHIPPED CREAM

Whipping cream (35% fat) 150 g

Castor sugar 1 Tbsp

Vanilla extract ¹⁄₄ tsp

CANDIED LEMON PEEL

Lemon 1, rind finely shredded

Water 80 g

Castor sugar 40 g

6. Pour lemon cream into baked tart shell and place in the freezer to chill for about 15 minutes.

7. Make whipped cream. Combine whipping cream, sugar and vanilla in a bowl placed over another bowl filled with ice cubes and water. Using an electric mixer, whisk cream at medium speed until stiff peaks form and cream is smooth. Spread whipped cream on chilled lemon tart.

8. Make candied lemon peel. Place finely shredded lemon rind in a saucepan. Cover with water and bring to a boil. Drain well. Return lemon rind to pan. Add water and sugar and cook over low heat for 5–7 minutes until mixture is syrupy. Sprinkle candied lemon rind with some castor sugar and dust off excess sugar using a sieve.

9. Garnish tart with candied lemon peel and chopped pistachios. Slice and serve.

strawberry tart

Makes one 20-cm round tart

Strawberries and blueberries 250 g

Neutral glaze 90 g

Water 25 g

SWEET SHORTCRUST PASTRY

Unsalted butter 70 g,
  at room temperature

Icing sugar 35 g

Salt a pinch

Vanilla extract 1/2 tsp

Eggs 20 g

Ground almonds 20 g

Pastry flour 130 g

PASTRY CREAM

Pastry flour 10 g

Cornflour 10 g

Fresh whole milk 200 g

Vanilla bean 1/2, pod split and
  seeds scraped

Egg yolks 3

Castor sugar 50 g

Unsalted butter 20 g

Kirsch (cherry liqueur) 1 tsp

1. Make sweet shortcrust pastry. Beat butter, icing sugar, salt and vanilla
   with an electric mixer until just combined. Add eggs and beat well.
   Add ground almonds and mix well. Add flour and fold through completely.
   Using a scraper, mix until a smooth dough is formed.

2. Place dough on a non-stick baking mat. Cover surface with cling wrap
   and roll out into a 3–5-mm thick sheet. Transfer to a tray and refrigerate
   for about 30 minutes. Remove non-stick baking mat and place dough
   (with cling wrap still intact) into a 20-cm fluted tart tin with a removable base.
   Press dough gently into tin without stretching it. Remove and
   discard cling wrap.

3. Roll a rolling pin over the top of the tin to remove excess dough. Prick dough
   with a fork and let rest for 5 minutes in the freezer.

4. Preheat oven to 180°C. Place some parchment paper or a non-stick
   baking mat over dough. Place baking weights into tart tin and bake for
   20 minutes. Remove weights and parchment paper or baking mat when
   pastry just begins to colour around the edges and continue baking for
   another 10 minutes until light golden brown. Remove from heat and leave
   to cool on a wire rack.

5. Make pastry cream. Sift flour and cornflour together twice. Place milk,
   vanilla pod and seeds in a saucepan and bring to a boil. In a clean bowl,
   beat egg yolks and sugar until pale. Add flour mixture and mix well. Add
   hot milk and fold through. Remove vanilla pod and pour mixture into
   saucepan. Bring to a boil over high heat, stirring constantly with a whisk until
   mixture is smooth and glossy. Remove from heat and stir in butter. Mix well.

STRAWBERRY CREAM

Castor sugar 45 g

Cornflour 15 g

Strawberry purée 180 g

NOTE: Replace the strawberry purée with mango purée, and the berries with mango cubes to make a mango tart.

6. Transfer pastry cream to a tray. Cover with cling film and place in a freezer to cool, but not freeze it. Before use, gently beat cream with an electric mixer until smooth and creamy. Add Kirsch and mix well.

7. Place cream in a piping bag fitted with a 1-cm round piping tip. Set aside.

8. Make strawberry cream. Combine sugar and cornflour. Add strawberry purée and sugar mixture to a saucepan and mix thoroughly. Bring to a boil over medium-high heat, stirring constantly with a whisk until mixture is thick. Remove from heat. Transfer strawberry cream to a bowl and place over another bowl filled with ice cubes and water. Leave cream to cool.

9. Pour strawberry cream into tart shell and spread evenly. Pipe pastry cream over and arrange berries on top.

10. Place neutral glaze and water in a saucepan. Bring to a boil, stirring constantly. Brash glaze on berries while glaze is hot. Slice and serve immediately.

chestnut tart

Makes one 20-cm round tart

Water 70 g

Castor sugar 35 g

Steamed shelled chestnuts 130 g

Rum 1 Tbsp

SHORTCRUST PASTRY

Unsalted butter 60 g,
cut into small cubes

Pastry flour 100 g

Salt ¹/₈ tsp

Castor sugar ¹/₄ tsp

Iced cold water 50 g

CHESTNUT CREAM

Chestnut paste 200 g

Icing sugar 30 g

Rum 1 Tbsp

Unsalted butter 50 g,
at room temperature

Egg 40 g

Egg yolks 3

1. Prepare chestnuts a day in advance. Place water and sugar in a small saucepan and bring to a boil. Add chestnuts and rum and leave to soak overnight. The next day, cut 100 g chestnuts into small pieces. Reserve remaining chestnuts for topping. Set aside.

2. Make shortcrust pastry two days in advance. Combine butter, flour, salt and sugar in a plastic bag and place in the freezer overnight. The next day, using a food processor, pulse mixture until it resembles coarse breadcrumbs. Add water and mix until dough is formed.

3. Place dough on a floured work surface and knead lightly. Put it into a plastic bag and refrigerate overnight.

4. Preheat oven 200°C. Prepare a 20-cm fluted tart tin with a removable base.

5. Place dough on a floured work surface and roll out to a thickness of about 5 mm. Brush away excess flour and place dough over tart tin. Gently press dough into side and bottom edges of tin. Roll a rolling pin over top of tin to trim edges. Prick dough with a fork and let rest for 5 minutes in the freezer.

6. Place a sheet of aluminum foil or a non-stick mat over chilled dough (without covering edges of dough), and press it well into the bottom edges. Place baking weights into tart tin and bake for 20 minutes. Remove weights and aluminium foil when pastry just begins to colour around the edges and continue baking for another 10 minutes until light golden brown. Remove from heat and leave to cool on a wire rack.

7. Make chestnut cream. Place chestnut paste, icing sugar and rum in a food processor and blend well. Add butter and mix well. Add egg and

WHIPPED CREAM

Whipping cream (35% fat) 120 g

Castor sugar 2 tsp

Rum 1 tsp

NOTE: This shortcrust pastry tart shell can also be used to make any sweet or savoury tart.

egg yolks and blend until thoroughly combined. Pour into a bowl and add 100 g chopped chestnuts. Mix well. Pour cream into prepared tart shell and level with an offset spatula.

8. Bake for 30–40 minutes. Remove from heat and leave on a wire rack to cool.

9. Make whipped cream. Combine ingredients in a clean bowl, then place bowl over another bowl filled with ice cubes and water. Using an electric mixer, whisk cream at medium speed until stiff peaks form and cream is smooth.

10. Spoon cream on cooled tart. Top with reserved chestnuts. Slice and serve.

coconut & raspberry meringue

Makes about 200 small pieces

COCONUT MERINGUE

Egg whites 75 g

Icing sugar 150 g

Finely grated coconut 30 g

Gold dust

Sprinkles

RASPBERRY MERINGUE

Egg whites 75 g

Icing sugar 150 g

Red icing colour a little

Freeze-dried raspberries

NOTE: This recipe will come in handy whenever you have excess egg whites. Meringue can be eaten on their own and can also be used to decorate othert desserts.

1. Preheat oven to 100°C. Line a baking tray with parchment paper.

2. Make meringue. Place egg whites in a clean bowl and beat with an electric mixer until foamy. Add a quarter of icing sugar and beat for a few minutes. Add remaining icing sugar gradually and beat until stiff peaks form and meringue is glossy.

3. For coconut meringue, add grated coconuts and mix well. For raspberry meringue, add a little red icing colour and mix well.

4. Spoon meringue into separate piping bags each fitted with a star piping tip. Pipe meringue into 2–3-cm long shapes onto prepared baking tray.

5. Sprinkle gold dust on coconut meringue and freeze-dried raspberries on raspberry meringue.

6. Bake for about 2 hours. Remove from heat and leave on a wire rack to cool completely.

7. Store in an airtight container with desiccant to absorb any moisture.

chocolate heart cookies

Makes about 40 cookies

Pastry flour 150 g

Cocoa powder 10 g

Unsalted butter 150 g,
 at room temperature

Icing sugar 75 g

Salt a pinch

Vanilla extract 1/4 tsp

Egg white 35 g (about 1 egg)

Whipping cream (35% fat) 20 g

Coating dark chocolate 200 g, chopped

Sprinkles

Freeze-dried raspberries

NOTE: For plain butter cookies, replace
cocoa powder with pastry flour, reduce icing
sugar to 70 g and add 1 tsp vanilla extract.
Plain butter cookies can be dipped in coating
white chocolate.

1. Preheat oven to 160°C. Line a baking tray with parchment paper.

2. Sift flour and cocoa powder together twice. Set aside.

3. Place butter, icing sugar, salt and vanilla extract in a bowl and beat with an electric mixer until light and creamy. Add egg white gradually and beat well. Add whipping cream and mix well. Add flour and cocoa mixture and fold in completely.

4. Spoon dough into a piping bag fitted with a star piping tip and pipe heart shapes onto it.

5. Bake for 20–25 minutes. Remove from heat and place on a wire rack to cool.

6. Place chopped coating dark chocolate in a bowl and melt over a double boiler. Dip one side of cookies in melted chocolate, then decorate with sprinkles and freeze-dried raspberries. Leave to dry on a lined baking tray.

7. Store cookies in an airtight container with a desiccant. Cookies will keep for up to 2 weeks.

gingerbread cookies
Makes about 20 large cookies

Unsalted butter 90 g,
   at room temperature

Brown sugar 80 g

Salt $^1/_8$ tsp

Vanilla extract $^1/_2$ tsp

Ground ginger $^1/_2$ Tbsp

Ground cinnamon $^1/_2$ tsp

Ground allspice $^1/_8$ tsp

Eggs 25 g

Molasses 30 g

Pastry flour 200 g, sifted

ICING

Icing sugar 125 g

Egg whites 20 g

Lemon juice as needed

NOTE: Use different cookie cutters for different seasons! For Christmas, use festive cookie cutters in the shape of gingerbread men, wreaths or stockings. At other times, use other fun cutters.

1. Preheat oven to 160°C. Line a baking tray with parchment paper.

2. Beat butter, brown sugar, salt and vanilla with an electric mixer until just combined. Add ground ginger, ground cinnamon and ground allspice and mix. Add eggs and molasses gradually and beat well.

3. Add flour and fold through completely. Using a scraper, mix batter until a smooth dough is formed.

4. Place dough on a non-stick baking mat. Cover surface with cling wrap and roll out into a 5-mm thick sheet. Transfer to a tray and refrigerate for 30 minutes.

5. Remove cling film and cut out shapes using a cookie cutter. Arrange on baking tray.

6. Bake for 25–30 minutes. Remove from heat and place cookies on a wire rack to cool.

7. Make icing. Place icing sugar and egg whites in a bowl and beat until fluffy. Add lemon juice and mix until icing is of piping consistency. Spoon icing into a piping bag fitted with a small round piping tip.

8. Pipe icing on cookies and set aside for icing to dry completely before storing.

9. Store cookies in an airtight container with a desiccant. Cookies will keep for up to 2 weeks.

caramel ice cream

Makes about 650 g

CUSTARD

Fresh whole milk 300 g

Egg yolks 3

Castor sugar 50 g

CARAMEL CREAM

Castor sugar 75 g

Whipping cream (35% fat) 200 g

CARAMELISED ALMONDS

Almond slivers 100 g

Castor sugar 120 g

1. Make custard. Heat milk in a saucepan almost to the boiling point, then remove from heat and set aside. In a mixing bowl, beat egg yolks and sugar until a light emulsion is formed. Pour warm milk into egg mixture and mix well. Return mixture to the saucepan and heat very gently, stirring constantly until mixture thickens.

2. Transfer custard to a bowl and place over another bowl filled with ice cubes and water to cool custard.

3. Make caramel cream. Place sugar in a saucepan and heat until sugar is caramelised. Carefully add whipping cream while stirring until mixture is smooth.

4. Transfer caramel cream to a bowl and place over another bowl filled with ice cubes and water to cool caramel cream.

5. Combine cooled custard with cooled caramel cream, then churn in an ice cream maker according to the manufacturer's instructions. Transfer churned ice cream to a container and leave to freeze overnight.

6. Make caramelised almonds. Bake almond slivers for about 20 minutes at 160°C without preheating oven.

7. Place sugar in a saucepan and heat until sugar is caramelised. Add almond slivers and mix quickly. Pour mixture out on a lined baking tray to cool. Chop into small pices.

8. Serve ice cream in pre-frozen bowls and sprinkle with caramelised almonds.

astrological herbal treats

aries ♡ ginger spice cake

Makes one 24-cm square cake

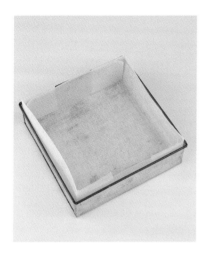  

Walnuts 60 g

Raisins 100 g

Pastry flour 210 g

Baking powder 1 Tbsp

Unsalted butter 100 g,
  at room temperature

Brown sugar 90 g

Dark brown sugar 30 g

Ground ginger 1 Tbsp

Ground allspice 2 tsp

Salt $^1\!/_8$ tsp

Honey 70 g

Dark molasses 60 g

Eggs 2

Sour cream 100 g

Whole fresh milk 60 g

Icing sugar 1 Tbsp

1. Bake walnuts for about 20 minutes at 160°C without preheating oven. Chop into smaller pieces. Boil raisins in a small pot of water and strain. Pat dry using paper towels. Set aside.

2. Preheat oven to 170°C. Line a 24-cm square cake pan with parchment paper.

3. Sift flour and baking powder together twice. Beat butter, brown sugar, dark brown sugar, ground ginger, ground allspice and salt until light and very fluffy. Add honey and molasses and mix well. Gradually add eggs and sour cream and beat well.

4. Add one-third of flour and fold in with a spatula. Add half the milk and continue to fold batter gently. Add another one-third of flour and fold in, followed by remaining milk. Add remaining flour, chopped walnuts and raisins and fold thoroughly.

5. Pour batter into prepared cake pan and bake for 50–60 minutes. Remove cake from pan and place on a wire rack to cool.

6. Dust cake with icing sugar and slice to serve.

21 March to 19 April

Strengths: Courageous, passionate, trailblazing

Weaknesses: Aggressive, short-tempered, selfish

Herb: Ginger. Ginger is good for digestion and circulation. It is effective in warming the body and helps alleviate mental stress.

taurus ♡ rose cupcakes

Makes 10 cupcakes

Pastry flour 120 g

Cornflour 20 g

Baking powder ¹/₂ tsp

Unsalted butter 100 g

Vanilla extract ¹/₂ tsp

Whipping cream (35% fat) 50 g

Milk powder 20 g

Hot water 1 Tbsp

Honey 15 g

Eggs 140 g

Castor sugar 130 g

Salt a pinch

ROSE JAM

Water 250 g

Dried rose petals 7 g

Castor sugar 175 g

Pectin 15 g

Lemon juice 50 g

PLAIN WHIPPED CREAM

Whipping cream (35% fat) 200 g

Castor sugar 1 Tbsp

Kirsh (cherry liqueur) ¹/₄ tsp

1. Make rose jam. Place water and dried rose petals in a small saucepan. Cover and bring to a boil, then reduce heat and simmer for 10 minutes. Mix sugar with pectin in a small bowl, then add to pan with lemon juice. Mix well. Continue simmering for 5 minutes. Leave to cool before using.

2. Preheat oven to 170°C. Line a muffin tray with 10 paper muffins cases.

3. Sift flour, cornflour and baking powder together twice. Place butter, vanilla and whipping cream in a bowl and heat over a double boiler. Once butter has melted, stir through to mix.

4. Place milk powder and hot water in a bowl and mix well. Add honey and mix again. In a clean bowl, beat eggs with a whisk. Add sugar and salt, then place bowl over a double boiler and mix well. When egg mixture is warm, beat with an electric mixer at high speed until light and fluffy. Reduce speed to low and continue beating for about 1 minute. Add honey mixture and mix well. Gently fold in flour, then add butter mixture and fold through evenly.

5. Spoon or pipe batter into prepared muffin tray. Bake for about 25 minutes until muffins are light golden in colour. Remove from pan and place on a wire rack to cool.

6. Make a small hole in the centre of each cupcake using a small spoon. Remove sponge and replace with 1 tsp rose jam.

7. Make whipped cream. Place whipping cream, sugar and raspberry purée (for raspberry whipped cream) in a bowl. Place bowl over another bowl filled with ice cubes and water. Using an electric mixer, whisk at medium speed until stiff peaks form and cream is smooth.

RASPBERRY WHIPPED CREAM

Whipping cream (35% fat) 200 g

Castor sugar 2 Tbsp

Raspberry purée 60 g

Kirsh (cherry liqueur) $^{1}/_{4}$ tsp

8. Divide both creams into 2 portions. Spoon into separate small piping bags and make a small cut at the tips. Place 2 piping bags (one plain and one raspberry) into a large piping bag fitted with a star piping tip. Pipe cream to decorate cupcakes. Repeat with remaining cream. Top with dried rose petals.

gemini ♡ peppermint chocolate cookies

Makes about 60 small cookies

Dark sweet chocolate (55% cocoa)
  50 g

Unsalted butter 120 g,
  at room temperature

Icing sugar 55 g

Salt a pinch

Pastry flour 160 g, sifted

Egg yolk 1

Peppermint tea leaves from 2 teabags

Granulated sugar as needed

NOTE: For a prettier presentation, the cookies can also be topped with fresh peppermint leaves. After baking for about 25 minutes, remove the cookies from the oven. Brush beaten egg whites on the back fresh peppermint leaves and place on top of cookies. Return to the oven to bake for another 1–2 minutes.

1. Place dark chocolate into a food processer and blend until fine.

2. Beat butter, icing sugar and salt until soft and creamy. Add egg yolk and mix well.

3. Add flour, peppermint tea dust and chopped chocolate to butter mixture and fold through using a spatula. Bring dough together in a ball and refrigerate for about 10 minutes.

4. Divide dough into 2 portions. Roll each portion into a log about 3 cm in diameter. Wrap logs with cling film and chill in the freezer. If not baking the cookies immediately, the dough can be kept frozen for up to 2 months.

5. Preheat oven to 160°C. Line a baking tray with parchment paper.

6. Slice cookie dough logs into 7-mm thick pieces. Roll edges of cookies in granulated sugar and arrange on prepared baking tray.

7. Bake for 25–30 minutes. Remove from heat and place on a wire rack to cool.

8. Store cookies in an airtight container with a desiccant. Cookies will keep for up to 2 weeks.

21 May to 21 June

Strengths: Adaptable, logical, multi-talented

Weaknesses: Restless, nosey, fickle

Herb: Peppermint. Peppermint is effective for digestion and helps release tension in the stomach. It can both warm and cool the body. It lifts the mind and calms the nerves.

cancer ♡ chamomile bavarois

Makes 8 servings

CHAMOMILE BAVAROIS

Cooking oil as needed

Fresh whole milk 200 g

Chamomile teabags 2

Egg yolks 2

Castor sugar 50 g

Gelatin sheets 10 g, soaked in iced water to soften

Apple juice 100 g

Whipping cream (35% fat) 200 g

CHAMOMILE JELLY

Water 200 g

Chamomile teabag 1

Gelatin sheets 8 g, soaked in iced water to soften

Honey 50 g

Lemon juice 1 tsp

Apple juice 100 g

1. Make chamomile jelly. Place water and chamomile teabag in a saucepan. Bring to a boil, then remove from heat. Cover and set aside for about 3 minutes. Remove teabag and add softened gelatin, honey, lemon juice and apple juice. Mix well. Pour jelly into a container and refrigerate until set.

2. Grease eight 80-ml moulds. Brush lightly with cooking oil and set aside.

3. Make chamomile bavarois. Place milk and chamomile tea bags in a saucepan and bring to a boil over medium heat. Remove from heat, cover and set aside for about 3 minutes. Remove teabags.

4. In a clean bowl, beat egg yolks and sugar until a light emulsion is formed. Add warm milk and mix well. Pour mixture into saucepan and cook over gentle heat, stirring continuously until mixture thickens. Add softened gelatin and mix through. Add apple juice and mix well. Strain mixture into a bowl. Place bowl over another bowl filled with ice cubes and water, and leave to cool to body temperature.

5. Place whipping cream in a clean bowl and place bowl over another bowl filled with ice cubes and water. Using an electric mixer, whisk cream at medium speed until stiff peaks form and cream is smooth.

6. Fold whipped cream into chamomile cream and mix thoroughly. Pour into moulds and refrigerate until set.

7. To unmould chamomile bavarois, dip moulds in warm water for a few seconds. Press edge of chamomile bavarois and invert on a plate.

8. Use a fork to break up apple jelly and spread around chamomile bavarois. Serve immediately.

22 June to 22 July

Strengths: Sympathetic, caring, highly imaginative

Weaknesses: Pessimistic, overly sensitive, moody

Herb: Chamomile. Chamomile aids digestion and ensures a good night's sleep. It eases anxiety, stress, anger and fear, and helps relax the mind.

leo ♡ rosemary orange galette bretonnes

Makes about 20 galettes

Unsalted butter 170 g,
   at room temperature

Icing sugar 90 g

Salt 1/8 tsp

Vanilla extract 1 tsp

Egg yolks 2

Ground almonds 30 g

Pastry flour 170 g

Fresh rosemary 5 g, finely chopped

Candied orange peel 60 g, chopped

EGG WASH

Egg yolk 1

Water 1/2 tsp

1. Preheat oven to 150°C. Line a baking tray with parchment paper.

2. Beat butter, icing sugar, salt and vanilla with an electric mixer until just combined. Add egg yolks and ground almonds and mix until just incorporated.

3. Add flour, chopped rosemary and candied orange and fold in thoroughly. (The dough will be very soft and sticky.)

4. Place dough in a plastic bag and roll out into a 1-cm thick sheet. Place on a tray and let rest in the freezer for about 20 minutes.

5. Remove chilled dough from freezer. Cut open plastic bag and peel away from dough. Place dough on a floured work surface. Use a 4.5-cm ring cutter to cut out as many rounds as you can from dough. Arrange on prepared baking tray.

6. Make egg wash by mixing egg yolk with water in a small bowl. Brush egg wash on surface of galettes, then score using a fork.

7. Place 5-cm ring cutters around each galette to help them keep their shape while baking.

8. Bake galettes for about 40 minutes. Remove ring cutters and place galettes on a wire rack to cool.

9. Store galettes in an airtight container with a desiccant. Galettes will keep for up to 2 weeks.

23 July to 23 August

Strengths: Creative, passionate, able to lead

Weaknesses: Arrogant, dogmatic, self-centered

Herb: Rosemary and orange. Rosemary is used for rejuvenation and helps enhance the memory. It aids blood circulation and strengthens the body. Orange warms the body and is effective for digestion. It lightens and energises the mind and refreshes the mood.

virgo ♡ lavender cream petit tarts

Makes 10 small tarts

Canned pear halves 2 halves, thinly sliced

Apricot jam about 50 g

SWEET SHORTCRUST PASTRY

Unsalted butter 70 g

Icing sugar 35 g

Salt a pinch

Egg 20 g

Ground almonds 20 g

Pastry flour 130 g

Dried lavender 2 g

SOUFFLÉ CUSTARD

Fresh whole milk 150 g

Dried lavender 1¹/₂ Tbsp

Egg 1

Castor sugar 50 g

Pastry flour 15 g, sifted

1. Make sweet shortcrust pastry. Beat butter, icing sugar and salt with an electric mixer until just combined. Add egg and beat well. Add ground almonds and mix well. Add flour and dried lavender and fold through completely. Using a scraper, mix until a smooth dough is formed.

2. Place dough on a plastic sheet or non-stick baking mat. Cover surface with cling film and roll out into a 3–5-mm thick sheet. Place on a tray and let rest in the freezer for about 15 minutes.

3. Prepare 10 tartlet tins each 8-cm in diameter.

4. Remove chilled dough from freezer and peel away cling film. Cut out 10 rounds using a 10-cm fluted round cutter. Gently press dough into tartlet tins and prick base with a fork. Place in the freezer for about 10 minutes.

5. Preheat oven to 180°C. Bake tart shells for about 20 minutes or until shells are light golden brown. Remove from heat and place on a wire rack to cool.

6. Make soufflé custard. Place milk and dried lavender in a saucepan and bring to a boil. Remove from heat, cover and set aside for about 5 minutes.

7. Separate egg. In a clean bowl, beat egg white until foamy. Add 30 g sugar and beat for a few minutes. Add remaining sugar and beat until stiff peaks form and meringue is glossy. Set a side.

8. Beat egg yolk and remaining sugar until mixture is pale. Add flour and mix well. Add hot lavender-infused milk and fold through. Strain and weigh mixture. It should be 130 g. If not, remove some milk or add milk to make it 130 g.

**23 August to
22 September**

Strengths: Analytical, capable, modest

Weaknesses: Overly critical, anxious, shy

Herb: Lavender. Lavender helps purify the mind and body. It is known to be effective in easing sleep anxiety. It balances the nervous system and stabilises the mind.

9. Return mixture to the saucepan and bring to a boil over high heat, stirring constantly with a whisk until mixture is thick. Remove from heat and add to meringue. Mix well.

10. Preheat oven to 180°C.

11. Spoon or pipe custard into tart shells and arrange 2 slices of canned pears in each tart. Bake for 25–30 minutes.

12. Place tarts on a wire rack to cool. Microwave apricot jam at 600 w for 30 seconds, then brush evenly over tarts. Garnish with dried lavender. Serve.

libra ♡ elderflower jelly

Makes 6 servings

Water 450 g

Castor sugar 75g

Gelatin sheets 15g, soaked in
  iced water to soften

Lemon juice 1 Tbsp

Elderflower cordial 90g

Canned or fresh grapes, peeled
  36 pieces

1. Prepare six 140-ml jelly moulds.

2. Place water and sugar in a saucepan and bring to a boil, stirring to
   dissolve sugar. Add softened gelatin and mix until dissolved. Add lemon
   juice and elderflower cordial and mix well. Transfer mixture to a bowl.

3. Place bowl over another bowl filled with ice cubes and water to cool
   jelly mixture.

4. Place 6 grapes into each mould and add 90 g jelly mixture. Place moulds
   in the freezer to set slightly.

5. Leave remaining jelly to set in bowl by placing the bowl over another bowl
   filled with ice cubes and water. Whisk jelly mixture to crush it, then pour
   over half-set jelly in moulds. Place in the refrigerator to set completely.

6. To unmould jelly, dip moulds in warm water for a few seconds. Press edge
   of jelly and invert on a plate.

**23 September to
22 October**

Strengths: Cooperative, sociable, sophisticated

Weaknesses: Indecisive, easily influenced, frivolous

Herb: Elderflower. Elderflower is a popular medicinal herb used to treat respiratory illnesses such as cold and flu. It is also effective for hay fever.

scorpio ♡ sweet basil orange muffins

Makes 6 muffins

Pastry flour 130 g

Baking powder 1 tsp

Unsalted butter 50 g

Castor sugar 80 g

Eggs 65 g

Sweet basil 5 g, chopped +
   6 leaves for topping

Milk 40 g

Orange juice 40 g

Oranges 2

CRUMBLE TOPPING

Unsalted butter 20 g,
   at room temperature

Castor sugar 20 g

Pastry flour 20 g, sifted

Ground almonds 10 g

NOTE: Muffins are best consumed within
1–2 days of baking. If not consuming
immediately, store in an airtight container
and refrigerate for up to 4 days or freeze for
up to 2 weeks.

1. Make crumble topping. Combine ingredients in a bowl and mix using fingers until mixture resembles coarse breadcrumbs. Place in the freezer until needed.

2. Preheat oven to 180°C. Line a 6-hole muffin pan with paper muffin cases.

3. Sift flour and baking powder together twice. Grate orange rind finely and set aside. Segment orange and place on paper towels.

4. Beat butter and sugar with an electric mixer until soft and creamy. Add eggs and beat until mixture is light and fluffy. Add chopped basil and grated orange rind and beat until well combined.

5. Add one-third of flour and fold in with a spatula. Add half the milk and fold batter gently. Repeat to fold in flour and milk. Add remaining flour and fold through, but do not over-mix.

6. Half-fill each cup with batter, then add an orange segment and top with more batter until cups are three-quarters full. Top with another orange segment and a basil leaf. Sprinkle with crumble topping.

7. Bake for 25–30 minutes or until muffins spring back when lightly pressed. Serve warm.

**24 October to
22 November**

Strengths: Clear sense of
purpose, resourceful, enduring

Weaknesses: Jealous, secretive, distrustful

Herb: Basil. Basil strengthens the nervous
system, sharpens sensitivity and
increases the level of concentration.
It also aids digestion.

sagittarius ♡ chicory & fig butter cake

Makes one 20-cm round tart

Dried figs 3

Dried cranberries 50 g

Pumpkin seeds 1 Tbsp

Apricot jam 50 g

SHORTCRUST PASTRY

Unsalted butter 60 g,
  cut into small cubes

Pastry flour 100 g

Salt $^1/_8$ tsp

Castor sugar $^1/_4$ tsp

Iced water 50 g

CHICORY ALMOND CREAM

Unsalted butter 90 g,
  at room temperature

Castor sugar 90 g

Vanilla extract 1 tsp

Chicory powder 10 g

Ground almonds 90 g

Cornflour 10 g

Eggs 90 g

1. Make shortcrust pastry two days in advance. Combine butter, flour, salt and sugar in a plastic bag and place in the freezer overnight. The next day, using a food processor, pulse mixture until it resembles coarse breadcrumbs. Add water and mix until dough is formed.

2. Place dough on a floured work surface and knead lightly. Put it into a plastic bag and refrigerate overnight.

3. Preheat oven 200°C. Prepare a 20-cm fluted tart tin with a removable base.

4. Place dough on a floured work surface and roll out to a thickness of about 5 mm. Brush away excess flour and place dough over tart tin. Gently press dough into side and bottom edges of tin. Roll a rolling pin over top of tin to trim edges. Prick dough with a fork and let rest for 5 minutes in the freezer.

5. Place a sheet of aluminum foil or a non-stick mat over chilled dough (without covering edges of dough), and press it well into the bottom edges. Place baking weights into tart tin and bake for 20 minutes. Remove weights and aluminium foil when pastry just begins to colour around the edges and continue baking for another 10 minutes until light golden brown. Remove from heat and leave to cool on a wire rack.

6. Boil dried figs and cranberries in a pot of boiling water and strain. Pat well with paper towels and cut figs into small pieces. Set aside.

7. Preheat oven to 180°C.

23 November to 21 December

Strengths: Generous, frank, open-minded, sincere

Weaknesses: Irresponsible, capricious, impatient

Herb: Fig and chicory. Fig is efficacious in stopping coughs and helps with shortness of breath. Chicory is valued as a beneficent herb for the liver from ancient times.

8. Make chicory almond cream. Beat butter and sugar until just combined. Add vanilla, chicory powder, ground almonds and cornflour and mix well. Add eggs and mix until well incorporated, but do not over-mix. Add half the figs and cranberries to the cream and mix well.

9. Pour chicory almond cream into prepared tart shell and level with an offset spatula. Top with remaining figs and cranberries, and pumpkin seeds.

10. Bake for 30 minutes. Remove from heat and leave on a wire rack to cool.

11. Microwave apricot jam at 600 w for 30 seconds, then brush evenly over tart. Slice and serve.

capricorn ♡ beetroot cake

Makes one 15-cm round cake

Walnuts 40 g

Raisins 40 g

Canned red beetroot (red beets) 150 g

Pastry flour 135 g

Baking powder 1 tsp

Ground cinnamon 1/2 tsp

Ground ginger 1/2 tsp

Salt 1/8 tsp

Egg 1 (about 60 g)

Brown sugar 60 g

Odourless cooking oil (such as grape
    seed oil, corn oil and canola oil) 70 g

Yoghurt 50 g

CREAM CHEESE FROSTING

Cream cheese 100 g

Icing sugar 30 g

Lemon 1/2, rind finely grated

Lemon juice 2 tsp

Yoghurt 1 Tbsp

1. Bake walnuts for about 20 minutes at 160°C without preheating oven. Chop into smaller pieces. Boil raisins in a small pot of water and strain. Pat dry using paper towels. Set aside. Using a food processor, blend beetroot into a purée. Sift flour, baking powder, ground cinnamon, ground ginger and salt together twice.

2. Preheat oven to 170°C. Line a 15-cm round cake pan with a removable base with parchment paper.

3. Beat egg in a bowl. Add brown sugar and beat until light and fluffy. Add beetroot purée, oil and yoghurt and mix well. Add flour mixture, then place walnuts and raisins on top of flour and mix well together.

4. Pour batter into prepared cake pan. Bake for 50–60 minutes. Remove cake from pan and place on a wire rack to cool.

5. Make cream cheese frosting. Microwave cream cheese at 600 w for 30 seconds until softened. Place cream cheese and icing sugar in a bowl and mix well. Add grated lemon rind, lemon juice and yoghurt and mix thoroughly.

6. Spread cream cheese frosting over cake. Slice and serve.

22 December to 20 January

Strengths: Responsible, disciplined, reliable

Weaknesses: Rigid, condescending, obstinate

Herb: Beetroot. Beetroot improves the digestive system and eases constipation. It also helps improve liver function. Expect detoxification effects.

aquarius ♡ cumin cheese cookies

Makes about 70 small cookies

Unsalted butter 170 g,
  at room temperature

Ground Parmesan cheese 200 g

Salt 1/8 tsp

Paprika powder 1 tsp

Egg yolk 1

Pastry flour 200 g

TOPPING
Ground Parmesan cheese 50 g

Cumin seeds 50 g

1. Place butter in a bowl and beat until soft and creamy. Add ground Parmesan cheese, salt and paprika powder and beat with an electric mixer until just combined.

2. Place dough in plastic bag and roll it out into a 5–6-mm thick sheet. Place on a tray and let rest in the freezer for about 20 minutes.

3. Preheat oven to 160°C. Line a baking tray with parchment paper.

4. Remove chilled dough from freezer. Cut open plastic bag and leave dough on the plastic. Use a cookie cutter to cut out as many shapes as you can from dough. Arrange on prepared baking tray.

5. Brush with water and sprinkle with ground Parmesan cheese and cumin seeds.

6. Bake for 20–25 minutes. Remove from heat and place on a wire rack to cool.

7. Store in an airtight container with a dessicant. Shortbread will keep for up to 2 weeks.

**21 January to
18 February**

Strengths: Original, progressive, humanitarian

Weaknesses: Inflexible, disobedient, outrageous

Herb: Cumin seeds. Cumin seeds have been used to aid digestion from Old Testament times. It is said that the ancient Egyptians used cumin to cure headaches. Cumin relieves tiredness and raises motivation.

pisces ♡ maple coconut ice cream

Makes about 640 g

Whipping cream (35% fat) 200 g

Coconut cream 100 g

Fresh whole milk 200 g

Dark maple syrup 140 g

TOPPING

Maple syrup

Maple crunch sprinkles

1. Mix whipping cream, coconut cream, milk and maple syrup in a bowl.

2. Pour mixture into an ice cream maker and churn according to the manufacturer's instructions. Transfer churned ice cream to a container and leave to freeze overnight.

3. Serve ice cream in pre-frozen glasses and top with maple syrup and maple crunch sprinkles.

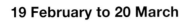

19 February to 20 March

Strengths: Compassionate, intuitive, adaptable

Weaknesses: Inconsistent, lazy, emotional

Herb: Maple. Maple syrup activates and supports liver functions. It has been found to contain polyphenols that have antioxidant properties and may help prevent cellular ageing.

weights and measures

Quantities for this book are given in Metric, Imperial and American (spoon) measures. Standard spoon and cup measurements used are: 1 tsp = 5 ml, 1 Tbsp = 15 ml, 1 cup = 250 ml. All measures are level unless otherwise stated.

LIQUID AND VOLUME MEASURES

Metric	Imperial	American
5 ml	$^1/_6$ fl oz	1 teaspoon
10 ml	$^1/_3$ fl oz	1 dessertspoon
15 ml	$^1/_2$ fl oz	1 tablespoon
60 ml	2 fl oz	$^1/_4$ cup (4 tablespoons)
85 ml	$2^1/_2$ fl oz	$^1/_3$ cup
90 ml	3 fl oz	$^3/_8$ cup (6 tablespoons)
125 ml	4 fl oz	$^1/_2$ cup
180 ml	6 fl oz	$^3/_4$ cup
250 ml	8 fl oz	1 cup
300 ml	10 fl oz ($^1/_2$ pint)	$1^1/_4$ cups
375 ml	12 fl oz	$1^1/_2$ cups
435 ml	14 fl oz	$1^3/_4$ cups
500 ml	16 fl oz	2 cups
625 ml	20 fl oz (1 pint)	$2^1/_2$ cups
750 ml	24 fl oz ($1^1/_5$ pints)	3 cups
1 litre	32 fl oz ($1^3/_5$ pints)	4 cups
1.25 litres	40 fl oz (2 pints)	5 cups
1.5 litres	48 fl oz ($2^2/_5$ pints)	6 cups
2.5 litres	80 fl oz (4 pints)	10 cups

DRY MEASURES

Metric	Imperial
30 grams	1 ounce
45 grams	$1^1/_2$ ounces
55 grams	2 ounces
70 grams	$2^1/_2$ ounces
85 grams	3 ounces
100 grams	$3^1/_2$ ounces
110 grams	4 ounces
125 grams	$4^1/_2$ ounces
140 grams	5 ounces
280 grams	10 ounces
450 grams	16 ounces (1 pound)
500 grams	1 pound, $1^1/_2$ ounces
700 grams	$1^1/_2$ pounds
800 grams	$1^1/_2$ pounds
1 kilogram	2 pounds, 3 ounces
1.5 kilograms	3 pounds, $4^1/_2$ ounces
2 kilograms	4 pounds, 6 ounces

OVEN TEMPERATURE

	°C	°F	Gas Regulo
Very slow	120	250	1
Slow	150	300	2
Moderately slow	160	325	3
Moderate	180	350	4
Moderately hot	190/200	370/400	5/6
Hot	210/220	410/440	6/7
Very hot	230	450	8
Super hot	250/290	475/550	9/10

LENGTH

Metric	Imperial
0.5 cm	$^1/_4$ inch
1 cm	$^1/_2$ inch
1.5 cm	$^3/_4$ inch
2.5 cm	1 inch